a BRAND new you

James Vince

DEDICATION

This book is dedicated to my mum.
You were the first person to ever believe in me.

ABOUT THE AUTHOR

Over the past 15 years I've started countless businesses, created 100+ brands in something like 20 countries. Some successful, others less so. But I've learned a lot about packaging and automating the process along the way. I have been a book publisher, a marketer, a chef, a graphic designer, a hedge fund manager, a burger king employee and now I'm an author.

After having my experiences with all these brands I've gleaned the secrets to learning, branding, building and growing a commercial idea. I have a proven and duplicatable formula for creating multiple, small revenue streams and growing them.

CONTENTS

ACKNOWLEDGMENTS

I want to thank my mother, for being the first person in the world to believe in me.

I would also like to thank my many employers and clients over the years, without whom, I wouldn't have gained this experience and been able to share it with you.

Finally.

Thank you for picking up this book and being part of my journey too.

1 THE FORMULA

Most people spend 40 hours a week, 30 weeks of the year, for at least 14 years, going to school.

We're told at age 13 that we have to pick a vocation. Something we will spend 40 hours a week, 50 weeks a year, for the next 52 years of our life doing.

That's a big responsibility for a 13-year-old. Which is why most people suck at life. Their whole life strategy was decided at 13.

I don't know about you but at 13 I was pretty smart and resourceful, I definitely didn't have enough experience to know what I wanted to do for the next 52 years though.

I've spent the last 20 years trying to figure exactly what I want to do with my life. People talk about your calling like you just know what to do in life and you just do it.

For some lucky people that may be the case, but at 13 I was 100% sure I wanted to be an astronaut. That dream died when I realised you had to fly planes first and in order to fly planes you needed to go to the best schools, pay crazy money and get straight A's for like 20 years.

I started my first business at 15, I knew from an early age I didn't want to work for someone, but life costs money so I decided I would try different jobs. A lot of jobs…

I worked in Burger King, Retail, I became a graphic designer, learned to code, a janitor in an art college, a chef, Mixologist, an English teacher, art teacher, Chief Technology Officer, Digital Marketing Specialist, Social Media expert, a professional artist, a book publisher and the list goes on.

Some with more success than others, but with every incarnation of my career, I would rise from the ashes of the last like a phoenix, learning new things about what it meant to be a professional.

Being a professional means you get paid to do something. Being paid to do something means you've convinced someone, you have enough expertise to help them solve a problem.

> To be a professional you need 3 things
> 1) Influence
> 2) Content
> 3) Kaizen (improvement)

You see, you can't be paid unless you can influence a person to think you're the right person for the job, you can't be the right person for the job, if you don't have content (the solution to their problem) and you can't stay making money if you never grow beyond the problem you just solved.

Whether you like it or not, when you help someone solve a problem, you give the solution to them. They have paid for the solution, Lawrence Blair once said, when enough people (monkeys in his case) are exposed to the solution, sooner or later it will catch on.

Just like Robert Kiyosaki did in the 90s when he told everyone "your house is not an asset unless you have cash flow from it". Today that's practically a meme. The value of this content has been diluted. You need to stay fresh to keep your value.

The average millionaire has 7 streams of income. The only way you can guarantee financial freedom is by increasing the value of your work or increasing the number of income streams you have. Increasing you the value of your work is possible, but it takes time. Something real and practical you can do today is, increase your income streams.

> This book will help you:
> 1) Define your transferable skills
> 2) Apply them to possible professions

3) Learn the foundational skills to get paid
4) Package and automate your solution
5) Repeat the process for another income stream

In this book are the tools you need to build a new, income stream every 3 months. Helping you make an extra $100 a month from a proven, duplicatable system that you can do over and over again until you reach your freedom number. The amount of money you need each month to become financially free.

It's such a simple concept, but few of apply it well.

I have had times in my life where I have either had or bought influence without first having content. The result is you can't solve the problem and you lose your influence. This is what people call over selling. This will lead to 1 of 2 outcomes. They will realise it's too good to be true and not buy form you or they buy from you and expect more than you can deliver. Either way that's not good. You could just be too early in your development of this profession to sell to that prospect(potential client). Every prospect has their stage. If you want to sell self-help products, you probably shouldn't try to sell to Tony Robbins, unless you're at a level where you can solve his problems. So you may have content, you may just be selling it to the wrong person. I'll help more with that later.

I have no influence but had content, which meant I could solve a problem for someone but nobody would believe me, which meant my branding wasn't convincing enough for them. This is the most dangerous position to be in. If people do buy from you, they will be left wondering why and if you don't meet what they think they should get for the money they won't be happy and probably won't pay. Maybe you sold yourself short to get the deal, which means you will be less motivated to work for less money, so the quality will suffer the result is the client will be less likely to pay you.

I have had influence and content, but soon got out of my depth when the problems I needed to solve evolved but I didn't. This is what I call when "the company outgrows you". Just like any relationship, one party can outgrow the other and you can also outgrow your company. When either happens, it's time to move on.

I give real examples of all of these later, how they've have affected my life and what not applying this formula has cost me.

Summary
It requires 3 things to be successful, Influence or the ability to convince people your idea is good, content; a solution to people's problems and finally you need to keep improving because the value of a solution degrades over time.

2 THE VALUE OF INFLUENCE

For the most part life is an interactive experience and interacting with other people or things will lead to one of three things, you will learn something new and change your actions, they will learn something new and change their actions or all parties will learn something new and change their actions.

If you want someone to buy from you (change their actions), you must share new information with them that gets them to change their actions (influence).

I am good web designer, I've been doing it for as long as I can remember. That in itself is not enough to convince you to buy a website from me. You want to know:

1.   What is it like to work with me?
2.   What support services do I provide?
3.   Will the quality be what I expect?
4.   Will I feel I've got value for money?
5.   If not can I get my money back?

All kinds of questions are yet to be answered.

But if I build a website that looks like this:

Figure 0-1 Not actually a picture of me :P

Then you see my portfolio of happy clients

Followed by testimonials from my fans

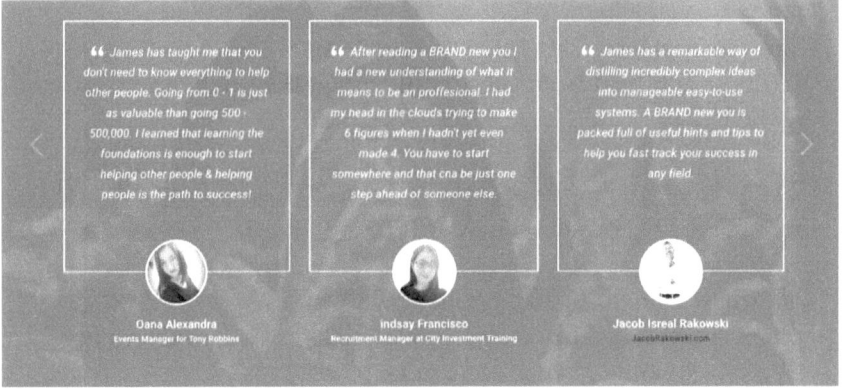

It gives you a better picture of what it's like to work with me. By the way none of the above are actually my website selling pages they're just examples.

I guess I started building websites for people professionally around 2005. A friend of mine had just taught me the basics of HTML & CSS and I had a loose understanding of WordPress.

I was electric with confidence and excited that my future was going to be all parties and beaches, now that I had a real trade people would pay for.

Now all I had to do was tell people I was in business and watch the money roll in. Right?
After just a few days of telling people I was in business I had 3 or 4 people asking me about websites and one of them wanted to pay me for a website! I was over the moon! But I'd never built a website by myself at this point. So I was a little nervous.

The guy was a typical type A Entrepreneur. This wasn't his first business and he'd been successful with at least one other website he owned§.

There was no sales process really, he sort of asked me if I could do a website for his business in WordPress. I agreed.

He wanted me to build custom additions to his WordPress called plugins, this was a bit over my head but I knew enough to get started, so I told I would have it done in just 5 days.

The first 5 days I spent just researching how to build these plugins and thinking I've got this, I just need to know how to do it.

After 2 weeks he contacts me and asks how I'm doing. My confidence disappearing I reply, yeah, um… everything's great, I just need to figure this last bit out.

A month and a half later I had to confess this was way out of my ability and he asked for his money back.

Did I have no business selling websites? Who was I to market myself as a web professional?

The truth is I just didn't influence the right person. I influenced a person who wanted something I didn't have a solution for at the time. There were plenty of people out there that wanted a basic website, something to get them started, but I just hadn't found them yet.

Before you begin any professional service make sure you and your prospect are 100% aware of what they are getting for their money so there are no nasty surprises for either of you.

You can offer professional services to people with only a basic understanding of the topic, but you have to find the people that will benefit from your help most.

This book isn't aimed at Mark Cuban or Deborah Meaden, they have years of experience and armies of branding experts on hand to help them with their next business.

What is more valuable a book that teaches you how to turn a $50,000 business into a $500,000 business or a book that teaches someone with who has never built a business before how to build their first business?

That depends who you ask.

Summery

I learned a valuable lesson. Influence and how you influence is important. The right kind of influence can make the difference between a job well done and confused client. But no matter how well you influence someone, the money won't last unless you have content.

Key Takeaways:
1) To be successful you must change people's actions
2) You can be influential or you can buy influence
3) Having influence alone will make you money, but not for long

3 THE VALUE OF CONTENT

You've probably heard the expression:
"if a tree falls in the wood and no one is there to hear it, does it make a sound?"

Having a solution to a problem but not being able to convince people pay you for it is a bit like that tree.

In the summer of 2013 I started yet another brand around web design. This time around, I think it was 5280 skills, a brand built around the fact that I was in Denver Colorado and the city is 5,280 feet above sea level.

The plan was to help young people learn coding skills and have them work for me and sell their services as an agency.

By this point my web design skills had come a long way. I could do this, I could teach these young people how to build websites, help them start their career and help other people start their websites too.

Great idea, but I didn't understand the American market and the solutions they need to their problems.

As a result the influence I had built up in the UK didn't seem to push the needle on Americans. They had a different value system, they had different wants and desires around a website and sure enough I couldn't seem to communicate my value to them.

I finally managed to sell a client on building him a website. We spent hours on that site, producing what I believe was a high quality, professional product that he would be happy to pay the second half of the invoice once it was finished.

So I did what I usually did at that time, I created a testing address (testing.hiswebsite.com), I put watermarks on the site and sent him the invoice with a note that said when the invoice is paid in full the site would be moved to the main address and the watermarks taken down.

His reply was quick and damning.

But his understanding was different. He told me to take down the website and to have my team stop working on it immediately. Demanding an immediate refund of the 50% down payment he had already given us.

Had I done something wrong?

You see when I sold him on our website services, using the words professional, high converting and eCommerce.

In my definition we had gone above and beyond that by adding a professional video with voiceover, a blog with 3 good sales copy posts based on keywords of his niche.

We never discussed design options, we never discussed what kind of photos he liked. How you sell a prospect on your services is vitally important. I go into more detail on selling in Chapter 12 (Automating the sales process).

Needless to say he no longer wanted to do business with us, I had an angry team of young professionals demanding to be paid for their work and the 100+ hours we put into his site was another lesson on the pile.

Summary

I learned a valuable lesson. Being able to provide the solution to someone's problem is great, but if you can't communicate that to the right people you have nothing. You might be able to get some success with content alone, but the world is full of broke people who can solve your problems.

Key Takeaways:
1) Content is king
2) If you want to be successful you must help people with their problems.
3) It's all well and good having a great solution, but if nobody wants to buy it from you it will be hard to be successful.

4 IN OVER MY HEAD

In early 2016 I started learning more about cryptocurrencies. I had previously been exposed to them from a friend of mine in London around the time they were invented. She even gave me one. Heaven knows what I did with it.

I learned about the history and became fascinated with them. It was exactly the sort of thing I would have been involved in from the start had the right person with the right kind of influence (☺) brought it to my attention.

In 2017 I applied for a job as "lead techie" in a cryptocurrency startup. Turns out what they really wanted was a Chief Technology Officer they had just had never hired one before. I'd never been hired as one before that, in truth I went home that day and had to look up what they did on YouTube.

I worked there for a few months providing some good value but at this point I realised couldn't continue to keep providing value as the company grew so I moved on.

I continued doing freelance work for other cryptocurrency companies, basic work, just low level but one of them was a reasonable enough name in the industry for me to get noticed.

I started going to trade fairs to get noticed more and meet people who needed my services. At the biggest trade fair in London, I was to run into friend I hadn't seen in around a year. He mentioned he was working on something big, and he needed my help, he just needed the funds to land then he would be in touch.

About 3 months later we met near the office he was using in his college to sell a cryptocurrency company on his services as a fund raiser. This guy was an example of the value of influence, he had convinced a heavily funded UK startup to part with £850,000 (GBP) so he could raise them £100,000,000.

Could he do it? He was 24 and this was his first ever project. But sure as hell he gave it a try, he hired a whole team of people with this money, all freelancers. One of them was me. He had hired me to write a technical description of what the client wanted to build.

About a month later the company was in trouble, many of the people they had hired could not fulfill on the tasks they had been assigned and it seemed like they would be unable to meet the agreement. The owners of the startup stepped in and asked him to give them what he had produced so far.

It wasn't a lot, the startup naturally asked for their money back and picked some of the people who had provided their value to come join the main team.

One of them was me. They saw I had been hired as a CTO for another cryptocurrency company, a competitor and they saw it as a great success poaching the competitions former staff.

I became their CTO for about 6 months, on a salary I had only ever imagined I would be capable of earning because I was providing value. I was the 3rd employee of the company and at the time I knew more about cryptocurrencies than the other 2 combined.

I would go to investor meetings, influencing them to invest more money into the company, I would help with marketing decisions, I built the brand of the entire company, all of the technical ideas came from me.

For someone who had never done this before I was sure doing well. I could think on my feet and I was creative. This is the most valuable asset an employee can have in my opinion.

Then they hired a new Chief Executive Officer (CEO, big boss), a more experienced one. He had experience running fortune 500 companies, and turning startups into mega companies.

He demanded results, and fast. With more money coming into the company we had to have someone like him onboard, someone who would give the investors what they wanted, product.

I was happy with my new role, I was the boss (of my department anyway), I was valued and I was compensated well for it. But he had other plans, he could smell my lack of experience and pedigree a mile off. He wanted nothing more than to fire me and replace me with someone double my age, with years of experience running companies 10 times this size.

As the pressure grew, I didn't rise to the challenge, I only knew part 1 and 2 of the formula, 1) influence people that you can do the job, 2) do the job. I was quickly becoming out of my depth and I could feel the need to move on again.

The pressure got too much for me in the end and I had to leave, I was naive to think I could just continue to
 provide the same content at the same value forever.

This is what I call the signal to noise ratio. It's the number of people capable of saying the same message as you (noise) out numbers number of people willing to hear your message (signal).

The amount of people who could do my job, for less than I was currently being paid, had grown to an accessible number that the company could approach them. My solution/content was devaluing by the day.

Summery

I learned a valuable lesson. Content is time sensitive. If you were selling fidget spinners in 2017 you would have made a small fortune because the patent applied for by its inventors in 1993 had just ran out. You could sell basic ones for a premium. If you were selling them in late 2018 however, you needed a gimmick to sell them, official Batman versions, custom designs and so on. Today so many people can make fidget spinners at super low prices that the number of people selling them has out grown the number of people who want them and the number of people who want them are declining. Signal to noise.

Key Takeaways:
1) The value of your solution degrades over time
2) You must constantly improve your solution
3) Your brand also has a limited life span
4) Entire industries disappear in time
5) The most sought after skill of the future will be the ability to see new trends, learn the foundations and become a professional

5 EVALUATING YOUR SKILLS

Before we can look at what Skills Abilities and Strengths (SAS) we have we need to know if we will provide the influence or the content. Yes, some people can do both, but usually people are better at one than the other. At this point it's probably good to define which one you are, because you can buy the other.

"The ability to deal with people is as purchasable a commodity as sugar or coffee and I will pay more for that ability than for any other under the sun."

John D. Rockefeller

If you currently don't have the budget to outsource the other then it is possible to do both, but long term you will have to look at choosing one.

I am better at content, which is why I don't film my own videos, promote my own courses or build my own promotional software, I use ClickFunnels for that, and I pay someone to use it for me.

Maybe you have so little influence you don't even want to be the face of your content, that's fine also, see if you can partner with someone who doesn't mind being the face of your company. Going to meetings, selling the product maybe they will be in the videos and on the website too.

Maybe you have amazing people skills but you just don't have anything you can sell. By the way there are millions of people who will pay you to teach them to be better influencers. As of writing, influencer courses are trending number one on Udemy, a popular online education platform.

But let's say you're not ready to package your own material right now, what can you do?

Well there are thousands of people out there that will do that work for you, and they don't even need to be your business partner.

You can hire ghost writers, people who create content for you, you can hire people to transcribe your audio and turn it into a book, you can hire people to build entire courses for you.

Some good places to start looking for people who can supplement your skills are:
1) Fiverr.com
2) Upwork.com
3) Freelancer.com
4) PeoplePerHour.com
5) Guru.com
6) TopTal.com
7) Themeforest.net
8) WriterAccess.com
9) TextBrocker.com
10) ClickBank.com

Either way, I recommend trying them both out if you can't figure out which one you are. Today it has become so easy to try different things that it's not a case of which one should I do but, which one should I do first!

Everyone has skills and abilities, chances are if you're an adult reading this book you have probably had at least one job where you provided some value for a period of time.

If you're not an adult yet you may have to rely on your strengths. Strengths are not the same as skills. A skill is something learn over time, you can develop it and learn new things about it. Your strengths are more about who you are.

Have you ever done something, that you didn't need much instruction on? For me it was riding a motorbike and driving a car. The first time I ever got in the driver's seat of a car I was 28. A good friend decided to teach me how to drive a car, in a car park (parking lot) in Boulder Colorado.

When I got in that car I was both excited and scared. But from the moment I knew where the gas and the breaks were, I was driving around the cars with ease and ready for the road.

For me learning how to ride/drive vehicles is a natural strengt. Not everyone knows their strengths, I still find it difficult when someone asks me to find a new strength.

For most people you can look at 10 things:
1) What did your parents do?
2) What did you always want to do as a child?
3) What do you people who don't like you compliment you on?
4) What would you do for free?
5) Which of the above do you like most?
6) Have you ever done something you needed little to no instruction?
7) If you have ever had a job, what did you like doing most?
8) Do you run fast, or swim fast or do anything physically well?
9) Are you physically creative, do you like painting or making things?
10) Do you remember a lot information or do well on tests?

If you already have a job, or like me, you've had many before, you can look at what we call transferable skills. Transferable skills are things you've learned at one job, that you have taken with you to your next job.

Not every job you do will be the exact same job. Even if you get promoted, you will have to tell your boss what you learned in your previous role that made you the right person for the new role.

Below is a chart of transferable skills and professions that could use those skills.

	Engineer	Sales	Musician	Builder	Lawyer
Engineer	x	Defining needs/Requirements	Structure	Reading technical documents	Passing tests
Sales	Product knowledge	x	Communication skills	Irregular hours	Customer Facing
Musician	Symbols	Improvisation	x	Use Technology	Good with words
Builder	Safety	Working to a deadline	Hand eye coordination	x	Working in a team
Lawyer	Studying	Negotiation	Self-Motivated	Time Management	x

The point behind this chart is not to make people change profession. It's to help you deidentify your skills and know that your skills and abilities are not limited to your profession.

Use the following chart to plot your skills and abilities.

This chart can also be downloaded from www.jamesvince.co/resources/

	Main Skill	Secondary Skill	Also used
College			
Job 1			
Job 2			
Job 3			
Job 4			
Job 5			
Other jobs			
Hobbies			
Work for friends			
Jobs for family			
Chores			
Other skills you may have			

The US department of labor lists about 100 industries on their website. It also drills down into a few possible jobs in those industries. But in my opinion this is a little outdated. I can't seem to find a comprehensive skills vs ventures database anywhere online. Which is why I'm working on one (visit jamesvince.co/skills to check if it's ready yet) it is not ready at the time of writing.

Today people seem to be making their own industries every single day. Today we live in a world of highly paid experts. Not because they have learned all there is to know about these existing industries but because they are in (Renée Mauborgne describes in her book) Blue Ocean Industries. There are no big fish in this industry yet, so it could be you.

In 2014 when Debbie Allen wrote The Highly Paid Expert, the were no experts teaching people how to become highly paid experts. So she became that expert. Today there are few people in the world who have explored and gained experience in as many industries, as quickly as I have, so I have branded myself as the guy who helps people be whatever they want to be in 3 months or less.

You are a creative person, whether or not you have exercised that muscle recently. You have the creative power to provide a new solution, something that no one has ever done before. You can be the new big fish in that very Blue Ocean.

Fortunately for the skills you don't yet poses there are thousands of websites dedicated to teaching you enough to learn the rest yourself and there are literally millions of people just waiting to take the jobs you don't want to do!

I talk more about learning new skills in The 12 Core Competencies and outsourcing in automating the process.

Summery

   Your skills and abilities are not limited to what you are currently doing. You have learned things that other industries are looking for, maybe even individuals. But before we can look at what is you should be doing, you need to know that there are other things you can do.

Key Takeaways
    1. You have skills you can apply to other areas
    2. You have natural strengths you just picked up quickly
    3. You can apply your strengths and abilities to get paid

6 VENTURE MATCHING

If you want to create a new venture, or add value to an existing one you will need to find a solution to a problem.

There are 4 things we use to build solutions
1) Our strengths
2) Our skills/abilities
3) Our knowledge
4) Creativity

A solution to a problem can be sold in the form of products and services. Remember anything can be a product and anything can be a service.

A product is solution you sell over and over again, usually without you having to provide the solution over and over again. For example teaching someone how to bake a cake. You can make a video of yourself making the cake, so you can provide that solution to people as many times as you want without you having to make the cake over and over.

Services and products can be 1 to 1, or 1 to many. But the whole point behind a product is that it can be sold to as many people as possible, time and time again. Creating a specific product over and over again, kind of makes it a service.

A service is an example of a tailor made solution that you apply directly to the people that need it.

Teaching a class is an example of a 1 to many service, you still have to be there to apply the solution, but you can apply that service to more than one person at a time.

Consulting with a client is an example of a one-to-one service. This usually takes up a lot of your time and you should probably only apply this solution to one customer at a time. This could include a company with the head of the company and his/her team, but typically you want to offer this to one customer at a time.

Then we have the one-to-many product version of a service. You can film yourself giving a class or giving a consultation session and then replay that to as many people as you like. Meaning it was a service, but it has no become a product.

A new type of solution is the Product as a Service solution, this is when you take a product, for example a series of videos and you limit people's access to it. You might for example charge $150 a month to gain access to all your products. But because it's time bound it's considered service. This is a service you don't have to be there to reapply over and over, maybe you have to manually open the product to them (you can automate this with software now days) but either way, you're not providing the service, you're just controlling access to it.

The combination solution

This when you take all of your collective experience and package it as one. Maybe you once worked in fast food, then after law school, you worked as a patent lawyer for a few years. The combination solution would suggest you provide consulting services for people wishing to get a patent on food production related inventions.

Discover you passion solution

Maybe you've been working for years at something you find soul destroying and you've always enjoyed making dolls for fun. You made them for yourself, your friends and anyone you knew that wanted them, for free of course.

Maybe you just couldn't bring yourself to charge people for something you feel is just a hobby. This is the perfect "discover your passion" solution as it's been hiding in plain sight all these years.

The fresh start

This is my specialty. When you just want to turn your back on everything you've done before and you just want to try something new.

Maybe you have no formal training or skills in this area, maybe you have some foundational knowledge or always admired people from a far who did it and you thought, "it's about time I get up off my butt and decide you want to learn how to _____".

Ultimately only you can know what your unique talents and skills are but you will need to develop the ability to coach people. As an expert it's your job to transfer your knowledge and experience to the client so there will be a degree of teaching and speaking skills involved.

You will no doubt have to sell yourself at least for the initial period, so having some sales skills or just being passionate about talking to people about what you have chosen to do is a huge plus.

When you're bringing a product to market, you need to consider the industry, which comes from the kinds people you want to help. The product is then decided by asking them their biggest problem and then all you have to do was solve it for them. Sounds simple right?

But when you are the product, you can't exactly build a fresh product to match what the client wants can you?

I'll cover this later but yes, you absolutely can.

Summery

When you look at the job descriptions of the solutions people are providing, you may find that you share a common skillset, you might even think you could do it better than them.

Recessions are great, because they highlight what solutions are being provided badly and even ones that don't fully solve the problem.

You can learn from that and provide the same solution in a better way or even make a much better solution.

Key Takeaways

1. There are many things your skills can be applied to
2. There are many types of solution, examples include;
    a. A solution you make or have someone else make that you sell to many people (a product)
    b. A solution you provide directly to a group of clients (Service)
    c. A solution you provide to one person or a group as a whole (Consulting)
    d. A solution you make or have someone else make that you sell to everyone but limit access to (Product as a Service)
3. Whether you're discovering a hidden talent, you're combining all your existing skills and experience or you're just trying something new there is a skillset every expert must master

7 THE 12 CORE COMPETENCIES

For most people, the idea of becoming an expert requires at least 3 years of professional school and countless other foundational requirements. Plus you may have to do many years of practice till you get it just right, and then maybe, just maybe you can start charging people for it.

The truth is to be an expert in something you just need to know more than other people about the topic. Unless you're the kind of person who wins every single general knowledge quiz at the local bar you probably don't have a broad knowledge of everything.

Right now there are millions of people preparing to search in some search engine "the super basics of x", and someone out there will be providing the super basics of x.

When I became an English teacher in Japan, I had to Google the answers to the entry questions. English is my first language, I did at least 13 years in some form of English spoken education, yet my knowledge of exactly how the English language was put together to form sentences, was not up to the level of being an English teacher.

After having Googled the answers to my test, I was amazed that the teacher agency wanted to provide my services to a public school! I've always been a very go-with-the-flow kind of guy so I saw this as yet another opportunity to reBRAND myself.

On the first day I was given 3 large English texts books (one for every grade in Japanese middle school). All of my predecessors had read these books cover to cover, had years of education and experience teaching English as a second language and here I was with no college degree, having only 3 bad months experience teaching in a private school, about to embark on teaching these kids English.

What right did I have to teach these kids anything, my understanding of the technical of the English language was probably not even as good as theirs. But determined to make a go of it, I decided I would read one lesson ahead of each of my classes, just one.

Every class I taught, I had read the text on that class just prior to going in to teach it. Did I feel like a fraud? Sure maybe on the first lesson, but after it went really well, I decided that I was providing value, because I was delivering the lesson, I knew enough to answer their questions and they enjoyed my lessons.

This is what people pay for, a solutions, support and to enjoy the process. If you have that solution, if you can provide the support they need, then you have matched the right audience with the right solution. This is the cornerstone of commerce.

Matching a solution to a need. The reason why so many people fail in business (I believe) is they try to match the wrong solution to the wrong problems.

If your audience is a group of electrical engineers and their problem is they need to go from expert to master level, providing a course in the basics of electronic safety probably isn't going to go down so well, but if your audience is 30 Japanese middle schoolers who have little knowledge of the English language and your solution is some knowledge of the English language and a whole lot of passion and inspiration to learn it, then this audience is gonna be happy with the solution you provide.

Becoming an expert in just three months is not easy, you can learn a lot in a month, but if people aren't willing to pay for that information, then you've wasted a month. So the key is to:

1. Find out what people are paying to learn that
2. Find out what key areas of competence you need in that area

Fortunately we live in a world were every single industry that exists is monitored by large corporations that want to sell to those people.

One of those corporations is Google and they collect a lot of information on what people are looking for, more importantly they keep track of what people buy!

A great place to start is Google Trends (trends.google.com), it shows you what people are currently looking for, the most popular times of year people look for it and even it allows you to compare one search topic against another.

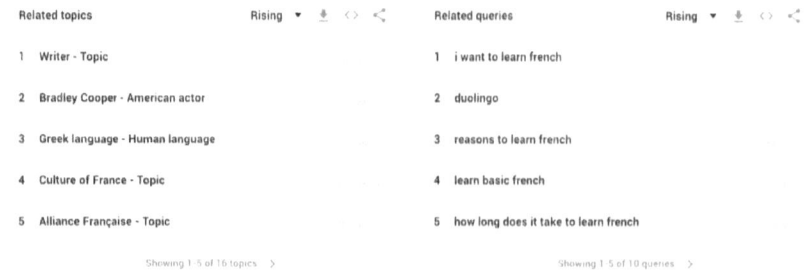

Related topics	Rising ▼		Related queries	Rising ▼
1 Writer - Topic			1 i want to learn french	
2 Bradley Cooper - American actor			2 duolingo	
3 Greek language - Human language			3 reasons to learn french	
4 Culture of France - Topic			4 learn basic french	
5 Alliance Française - Topic			5 how long does it take to learn french	
Showing 1-5 of 16 topics >			Showing 1-5 of 10 queries >	

Recent popular terms

As you can see the American actor Bradly Cooper is trending as of writing because of the song her collaborated with Lady Gaga to make, has become popular on YouTube.

People are searching for learning French 170% more than they were last month and it seems DuoLingo is the way they are doing it.

Having an app, that people love to use, is a great way to build authority and establish a personal brand (I talk more about this in Creating Content).

I personally speak English, Italian, Japanese and I'm learning Thai. Learning a language is a great way to keep your mind active, and pass the time when you're waiting for people.

Most people think that learning a language is super hard, but just like anything it can be broken down into 12 core competencies.

1. The script
   English uses Roman script, Japanese, Arabic & many others, don't!
2. The pronunciation
   Just because your language uses a silent E doesn't mean all of them do
3. Basic vocabulary
   Hello, My name is, how are you, I'm fine thank you
4. The conjugation
   In English we change the verb depending on the tense, in Italian they change the verb depending on who is saying it, for example I read "Leggo", they read "Leggono"
5. The basic verbs
   Run, jump, speak, listen, learn, do, be
6. The question starters
   Who, What, When, Where, Why
7. The translation
   How do I say this in my language? How do I say this in your language?
8. The glue
   Because, and, therefore, however, but,
9. The conditionals
   If then, else, for each, while,
10. Plurals
    Some languages don't have plurals, Japanese doesn't. English usually just ads an S on the end. Some languages are more complicated. For example: In Italian newspaper is "Giornale" newspapers is "Gionali"
11. The grammatical genders (if applicable)
    Some languages have more than one way to call nouns depending on if they are feminine or mescaline nouns. For example French and Italian. Greek, Dutch and German have 3 genders, Czech and Slovak have 4 (OMG right!).
12. The flow
    Depending on the rhythm, what you say can sound kind of odd. For example: The cat, ran down the, street with two, fish in, her mouth. If you say it like that it sounds weird

I haven't found a single topic you can't pinpoint 12 core competencies and apply yourself to solving them. That means that, in 12 x 1 hour sessions you can learn enough to move the need.

Does it mean that you know every single verb, every single noun, every single conjugation rule in just 12 hours?

Heck no, but it does mean that you will have a firm grasp of the foundations of any language.

If you know 100 words, you can talk to people, if you 1000 words you can stop learning from a book and rely completely from language use.

If you do this for Italian, in just 12 hours, I can promise you it's enough to start independent study because I've done it.
I took these 12 competencies (skipping number 1 of course) one hour on each, for 12 hours one hour per day.

After the 12 days I was able to study Italian with just a dictionary and a book on Italian grammar from there. Of course that doesn't mean I didn't include extra help. I used a website call ITalki to connect to 3 or 4 Italian language coaches once a week to help build on that for 3 months.

After just 3 months I was able to communicate with anyone in Italian, if I didn't understand what someone was saying, or they spoke in an odd dialect, I could simply explain to them that I didn't know that word yet and ask them to use a more simple way to explain.

Now I am conventionally fluent in Italian.

My example of teaching Japanese middle schoolers English with little to know understanding of the material is not exactly true. I am a native English speaker, which of course gave me the foundations I needed to grasp the text books I was reading. Had I never seen the English language before, this might have been impossible.

This is why I recommend the 12 key foundation competencies before you start applying your knowledge. You can do it with literally any topic, maybe you will need help to create the 12 competencies in your chosen profession, you will also need to work with professionals to act as your training wheels for some time, you may even need to work with mentors your entire career, but the point here is not to make you the best in the world, it's to get you confidently walking the path to becoming an expert.

Let's try it again with another profession, maybe one not as easily mapped out as learning a language, let's try becoming a life coach.

A quick internet search has taught me that there are a few things you need to master to become a life coach. They are; listening, creating strategies, asking questions, creating assignments, building trust, developing a growth mindset, goal setting, problem solving skills and the ability to change people's opinion (influence) to name a few.

So I think a reasonable 12 competencies might look like this:

1.	Mindset training
	Basics of Neuro Linguistic Programing (NLP), Cognitive Behavioral Therapy (CBT)
2.	Creating a vision
	learn the tools and skills necessary to get clear on what you want
3.	Learn goal setting techniques
	Specific, Measurable, Attainable, Realistic and Time Bound (SMART) method, Cascading goals, 4 quadrant goal setting
4.	Asking Effective Questions
	The PDST Method (Available at jamesvince.co/resources)
5.	Building Trust
	Again NLP, The Able, Believable, Connected, Dependable (ABCD) Method, Read "How to Win Friends and Influence People"
6.	Effective Note taking
7.	Inspire
	The Goal, Reality, Obstacles, Way forward (GROW) method
8.	Specific tools
	Check out Clever Memo, My Quest, Trello, Satori, Calender.ly, Assistant.to, Loom, Zoom, Hello sign and Evernote
9.	Life Balance Tools
	The wheel of life
10.	Personality types
	Myers Brigs, HEXICO, HOPE, DISC
11.	Public Speaking
	Toast Masters, Local meetups and acting classes
12.	Making Assignments
	Microsoft Word, Survey Monkey

I recommend you work with someone who is already doing your chosen profession before you build your 12 competencies. Maybe even have them help you build the list.

Putting together you 12 core competencies will help you plan out what competence looks like to you.

I believe that almost any industry can be broken down into 12 core competencies, and once you have mastered them, you can start putting them into practice.

Once you fully get the theory behind your topic you're going to want to test the waters. The way you do that is by working with people. For free. At this this stage you don't really have anything to offer them, only that you know a bit more than them (theoretically).

The best way to do this is to find a venue that will let you work out of there, ideally for free. Create a poster (Canva.com is great for this!) And print it at your local copy shop.

Then you're going to want to put it on Facebook, because Facebook lets you promote events for free.

Open facebook.com hit create in the top right corner, move down to event, and you should see something like this.

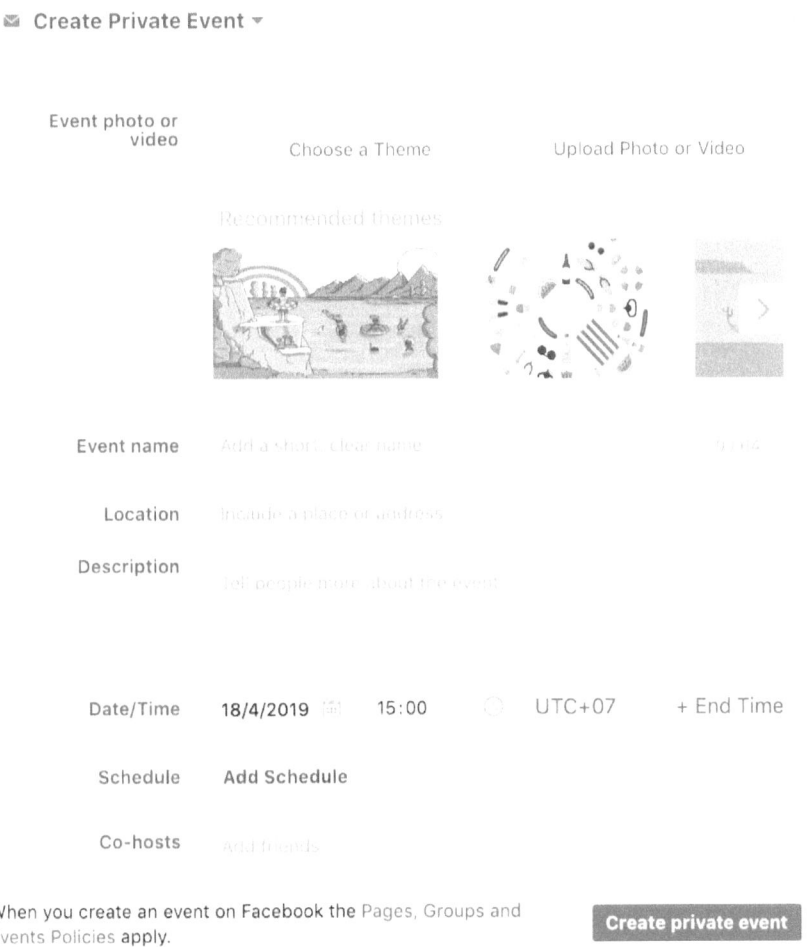

✉ Create Private Event ▾

Event photo or video   Choose a Theme   Upload Photo or Video

Recommended themes

Event name   Add a short, clear name

Location   Include a place or address

Description   Tell people more about the event

Date/Time   **18/4/2019**   **15:00**   UTC+07   + End Time

Schedule   **Add Schedule**

Co-hosts   Add friends

When you create an event on Facebook the Pages, Groups and Events Policies apply.

Create private event

Bear in mind Facebook changes all the time, so it might not look like this if you're reading this after 2019.

Click on private event and change it to public. It will ask you for an image (again Canva.com has a making for this!), fill in the event location and time and you have a live event on Facebook.

Try to find some Facebook groups you can post it in that might like your event, the more specific the better. For example an event in Brisbane for writers, you might wanna put that in the Brisbane Aspiring Writers group, but if the kind of thing you wat to help people with is not yet in Facebook, just post it in your area's events group. For example Chiang Mai events. There is a group like this for almost every major city. Tip, if there's not, just create the group.

Next you're gonna wanna head on over to EventBrite.com. It's free to post events on eventbrite and this video is a great guide for 2019. Again it may change depending on when you read this.

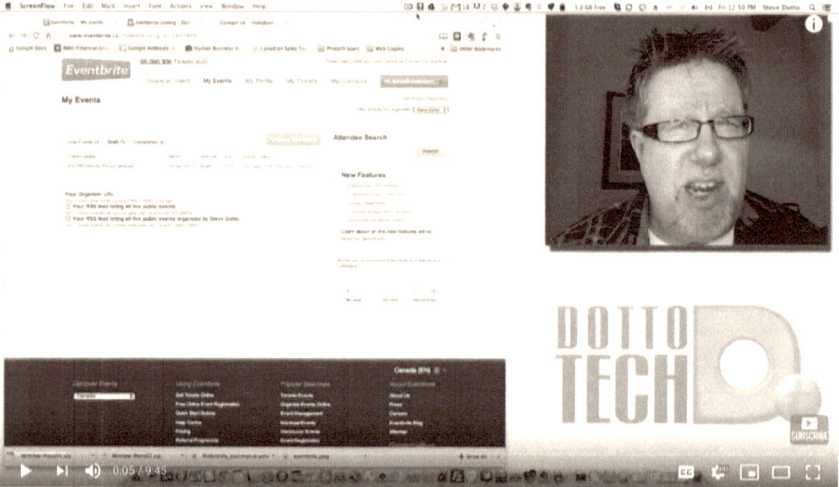

0-2 https://www.youtube.com/watch?v=bPDybu5orxs

Be sure to highlight to people that it's your first time, it's free and all you're looking for is their feedback. The people that do come, should be at a level where you can add some value to them.

During the event make them aware that it is very low level and if they feel they know the basics of your topic, this event might not be for them.

How to structure an event

When you first arrive greet the people arriving early, et to know them, ask them what their number one problems are with your topic, after all that's the whole reason you're putting on this event.

Start with an informal greeting session, give everyone the chance to say as much or as little about themselves as they'd like to.

I usually ask them to state their name, what brought them here, what their experience is with the topic and what they would like to get out of the event.

After that you want to spend some time explaining who you are and what your experience is with the topic. Be honest with them don't pretend to know more than you do and have fun with it.

Remember, it's ok that you're not much more along than they are. They're here for free and you know the 12 competencies, you are theoretically ahead of them because you have the core competencies down.

Talk to them for about 10 to 20 minutes about what you know of the topic, after each section remember to pause to give your audience time to answer questions.

When you are finished, thank them for coming and open the floor for questions, if you can't answer them, that's ok, write it down and tell them you will get back to them after.

Bring the event to a close by asking them to write their names and email address on a piece of paper and ask them if they wouldn't mind filling out a short feedback form, an example of this can be found on the next page.

It can also be downloaded from JamesVince.co/resources

Please let me know how you felt about the event	100%	75%	50%	25%	0%
Do you feel you have gained valuable knowledge?					
How useful was it to you?					
Did this event meet your expectations?					
Did you like the presentation?					
How good was the presenter?					
Would you pay for an event like this?	Yes			No	
If you answered yes, what would be a fair price?					

If you were to pay for an event like this, what question would you want it to answer?
Please use the space below to add any additional thoughts or information

Take what you learn from each event, your main goal here is to find out what people will pay for.

Make sure that after every event you read the feedback forms, learn from them and try to find the answer to their problems. This will form the content/solution you will sell to people.

Do this a few times until it feels comfortable and the you can answer their questions with ease.

Ok, so you have your 12 core competencies, 3 months or so of practicing this with real people and a much better understanding of what they want to pay for, you're ready for business, you just need a Minimum Purchasable Solution.

Summery

To prepare for business you need a knowledge and skillset to handle questions outside of the scope of your solution, this is how you provide support. We do this by breaking the topic down to no more than 12 core competencies. This makes you theoretically ahead of your potential customers, but to make a real difference you need to put it into practice.

Key Takeaways
1. Any solution can be broken down into 12 core competencies
2. You will need training wheels while your practice
3. Just 3 months of real world experience is enough to learn as you go

8 MINIMUM PURCHASABLE SOLUTION

So you've spent the last 3-4 months learning the core competencies. Now you need to provide your new solution. What exactly does a solution look like?

A solution can be broken into parts. Just like you brake down a problem to solve it, you can also break down a solution to deliver it. You can start with a simple part of the problem.

For example if the problem is learning a language. A PDF of the top 50 Italian verbs is going to solve part of that problem. You might be able to give that away for free.

The next part might be an MP3 series of a native speaker saying the most common words or phrases.

The next an introduction to Italian course and so on.
Breaking up your solution like this not only allows you to meet people where they're at and provide the right solution, but also allows you to maximise the return on your hours invested.

To make this work in a scalable way, you will need a combination of all four solution types.
1. A product (Low value, low price)
2. A one-to-many service (Medium value, medium price)
3. A Product as a Service (High value, great security)
4. A one-to-one Service (Highest value, highest price)

As an expert who plans to automate their business, this usually looks like this:
1. One or more training videos, books, MP3s, affiliate products
2. One or more webinars, retreats
3. Coaching programs, training video libraries, mailing list subscriptions, affiliate products
4. Consulting

For example I have training courses you can purchase on a one off basis, you bought this book and that's a product, I run monthly elite BRANDers coaching sessions every month for up to 30 people, I run private coaching sessions and you can also get access to all my online coaching programs for one monthly price.

You can include a Facebook group as part of the package but Facebook's rules state that you can't charge people for access to a group (although people do).

You can even do it before have the full product. This book was on sale for a whole month before you could buy it. Using Amazon's pre-order function, you can sell almost any product without actually having the product first.

Of course you have to make sure you can actually provide the solution on the date you say you will provide the solution.

As of writing I have created 3 courses for my website
1. Own your life
2. Learn anything in 12 hours
3. A BRAND new you (the course accompanying this book)

Creating a course

Creating a course is like taking someone on a journey. You have to relate to your audience, you need to let them know that you were once where they are.

You have to show them the inspiration for change, you have to show them the benefits of change, you have to show them the change, you have to show them your setbacks, you have to show them the results of the change, you need to show them how you enforce the change and finally you need to show them how the change has affected you.

After going through your course, the customer has to have gone through all the steps that you took to get where you are now, but in less time. They have paid you to help them cut the learning time. This journey has to result in them having the same results as you have by the end of it or they will either feel cheated and want their money back or they won't participate in your course or review it.

The following is a chart you can use to help make your course

Before I learned to _____	The reason I learned to _____
• Key point number 1	• Key point number 1
• Key point number 2	• Key point number 2
• Key point number 3	• Key point number 3 •
What I learned was _____	While I learned to _____
• Key point number 1	• Key point number 1
• Key point number 2	• Key point number 2
• Key point number 3 •	• Key point number 3 •
The hardest thing about _____	Now I can _____
• Key point number 1	• Key point number 1
• Key point number 2	• Key point number 2
• Key point number 3	• Key point number 3
I stay on track by _____	No I enjoy _____
• Key point number 1	• Key point number 1
• Key point number 2	• Key point number 2
• Key point number 3	• Key point number 3

I recommend one video per topic maybe if the video runs a bit long you can have a part I and a part II. You wanna keep them typically no less than about 7 minutes each, if you're not super charismatic on camera, I recommend trying to keep them under 20 minutes or they might start to get too board.

For tips on being more engaging on screen check out my friend Charlie from Charisma on Command:
https://www.youtube.com/user/charismaoncommand

Once you create your course content you're going to need to record yourself providing the solution. How you do this will depend a few things:
1. Will you demonstrate with a computer screen?
2. Will you demonstrate with a white board or other props?
3. Will you demonstrate with other people in a live audience?

If you only need yourself and a presentation document you can use a webcam and a screen recorder such as:
1. Cam Studio (Open Source and free)
2. EzVid (Free)
3. Smart Pixel (Not Free, Not easy to use)
Some mac examples include:
1. Quicktime (Free)
2. ScreenFlow
3. SnagIt ($50 USD)
4. Camtasia ($249 USD)

When you have your screen recording software open, open your camera software and resize it so that it's not in the way of your presentation.
   If you need props such as a whiteboard or others it might be possible for you to just buy a tripod and point the camera at yourself.

A few good cameras I recommend are:
1. Canon PowerShot G7 (Inexpensive and a great camera $249)
2. Cannon EOS 77D (Really expensive at nearly $650 USD but my personal choice)
3. Sony A6000 (Mid-range high quality camera $500 USD)

If you need to work with other people, you may need to hire someone else to do the filming for. You'll need them to capture the questions, the reactions and the moments that make the experience immersive.

Editing the videos

Having really high quality video editing can make the difference between a great course and an amazing course. You can impact people and provide value, from videos that are raw and in edited if you have good content but they're are to watch longer and share it with all their friends if they enjoyed the videos.

I get it, video editing seems like another 12 competencies right there but you can learn as you go. You don't need to study video editing to do this.

But for those of you who wish to take your videos to the next level and make them super flashy I highly recommend you check out this video course on iMovie editing by Rafi Saar:

https://www.udemy.com/the-complete-imovie-course/

The key elements of editing a video are:
1. Make an intro
2. Transitions
3. Make an outro

An intro is the short 2-5 second introduction that has either your logo or your core message with some nice effect on it. This is played at the beginning of every video, so people know they're on a video from you.

We put transitions in place to smoothly lead you away from one edit to another. You might make mistakes in your videos, so you may have to cut bits out. This will lead to the rhythm of the video being changed. It might come to a sudden stop in talking or your hands might not be in the same place as before the cut.

A transition can take the old image and sound and blend it smoothly with the new clip after the cut.

An outro is exactly the same as an intro by on the way out. This could be the same if you just want to display your brand, or it could be just a call to action if your intro was more complex.

A great example of an intro, transitions and an outro can be found on my buddy Mike Vistil's YouTube Videos.

Figure 0-3https://www.youtube.com/watch?v=9jPv16olc0o
He pays the same 15 second clip of him walking through exotic locations, doing backflips playing the ukulele in is expensive villa and generally having a good time.

You can also outsource the editing of the videos, making the intros and the outros and I highly recommend you do if you have the budget because it can become really time consuming.

A great place to start is Fiverr.com

Supplemental resources

You could just upload videos and have people watch them, but for them to feel like they have got true value from your course you should offer print outs, exercises and maybe even MP3 downloads to make your course more valuable.

Great examples of this is worksheets, you can help people get closer to finding a solution by writing down their problems in a functional way.

This is usually a table with a heading and maybe some side headings and the rest is left for them to fill out. Like some of the print outs in this book.

You can use MP3s to add extra clarity, maybe something couldn't be fit into the original course material but you feel like it could support the learner by giving them extra context which is outside the scope of the course.

Delivering your video

So there are two ways you can do this, you can build a website and provide the courses yourself like I have. This is great because it gives you full control over your content. When the course is available, to whom, for how much, you get the idea.

When you use a 3rd party website to deliver you course you risk losing control over all of that. They can have flash sales, you may have to share a small piece of the overall pie from all monthly subscriptions and they can cancel your account at any moment if they don't feel like you align with their guidelines.

For now, to get yourself started, I recommend having companies deliver your courses for you. It's less work, they handle the sales side of things and you can get started today.

A couple of examples include:

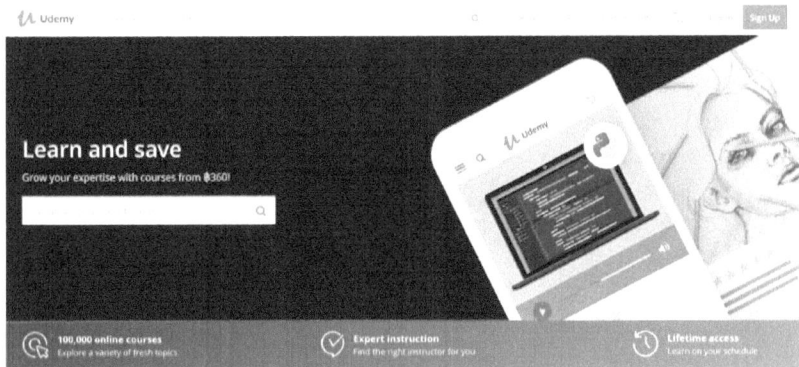

Udemy.com

Udemy is a great website creating stand-alone courses you personally get the money for.

The benefits of using Udemy are that, they already have a large audience wanting to learn, they let you set your own price for the course (recently capped at $50 USD) and they let you upload supporting material.

The drawbacks to Udemy are they charge you 50% of the course fees if sold at full price and 3% if sold in one of their promotions which usually brings it down to only about $11 USD.

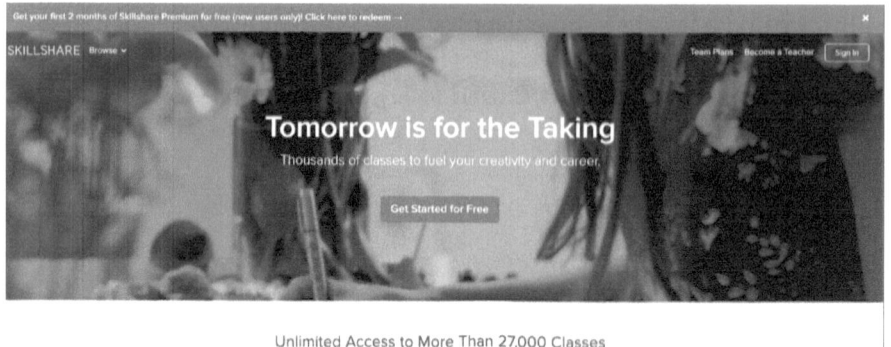

Unlimited Access to More Than 27,000 Classes

Skillshare.com

SkillShare is a great course host, with 8 million users and growing fast. It's not hard to see why people would use them to host their courses. They do most of the marketing so you don't have to, people already pay to be a member of the site so taking your course costs them no extra.

On the downside they have to pay no extra to take your course. The total membership is divided by the amount of viewed seconds that each instructor has had. Meaning someone might sign up for your course but never use it. If this happens you get no money.

Some people might argue that's the way it should be, that if you don't use it you don't pay for it. But that's not really far on the instructor who has put hours of his/her life into making this course and sees nothing in return.

Plus even if they came to SkillShare from your signup page they could still be distracted by the other courses on offer, they paid to get access to at the same time as yours.

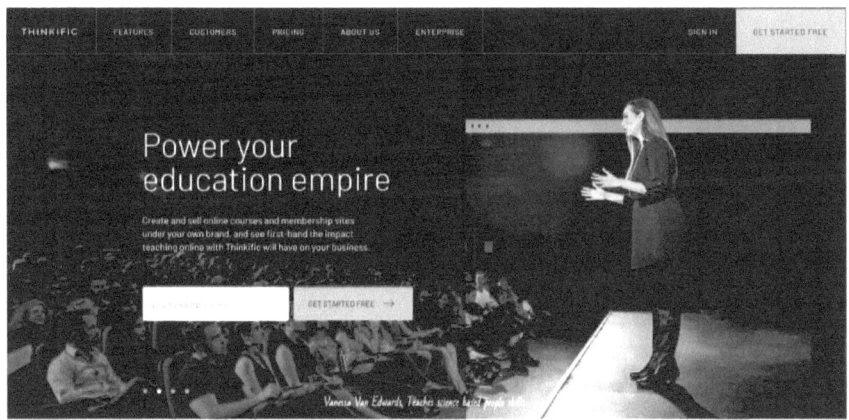

Thinkific.com

Thinkific is hands down the best option for a beginner. It allows you to submit 3 courses, Have unlimited students and your own private course are.

The only downside to Thinkific is the fees. They seem to take more than 2/3 of the revenue of your course and give it to themselves, charity, affiliate partners and heavens knows who else.

Maybe this changes if you buy the higher tier packages but from what I've read it doesn't seem to.

Another option for delivering your courses is hosting it yourself. This can be done for as little as $69 with WordPress and an extension program we call a Learning Management System (LMS).

Here's a list of some good LMS for WordPress:
1. LearnDash
2. LifterLMS
3. LearnPress
4. Sensei LMS

If you Google any of them they will be the top link.

Of course you can pay someone to make a website for you too.

9 WHO IS IT ALL FOR?

You're about to provide a solution. But who exactly buys what you want to sell?

Your solution is amazing. That means everyone will want it right?

Well not exactly. There's 3 reasons not everyone will want your solution:

1. They might not need it (hard as that may seem)
2. They might not be able to afford it
3. They might not like it

Ok, so let me explain this before you all turn around and lynch me lol.

Need

If you're trying to teach people how to become a fisherman/woman, then someone who is pathologically scared of being on any body of water, may not need your solution.
If you're selling an introduction to US law, someone who has already passed the bar defiantly doesn't need it.

Afford

It seems harsh to say but people who can't afford your product shouldn't have access to it. Partly because you've spent hours of your life creating that solution and you need to be compensated for it.

Remember a solution doesn't last long, sooner or later I will have to write a version 2 of this book because the information will become outdated, someone could rip it off or (and this is my personal favourite) you all could have read it and now nobody else needs to know it.
You can hold flash sales for those who can't afford your products, but it's proven that if someone doesn't invest something to get a course that requires input, they won't put in the work.

If you let someone have access to your solution for less than it's worth, they won't value it and won't fully utilize it to its fullest.

Also you'll have a range of products people can use, ranging from free to crazy high, but I'll go over that more in later chapters.

Like

Some people will see need your solution, see your solution, maybe even buy your solution, but still hate it.

Can you believe that? Someone would go all the way to buying your solution and not love it? There will be some people who won't like this book (hopefully I will have branded and marketed it well enough so that's not many people) but that's ok, I'm not for everyone and nor should you be.

Just be prepared for that fact that even people who buy your solution may not like it.

If you're doing your job properly in branding and marketing then that should be less than 5% of people who buy.

Also you don't want to market to everyone because the marketing budget would be huge, imagine getting an ad to be shown to every single person on Facebook, that's crazy right?

Ok So we've established our solution isn't for everyone.
So who is it for?

We can find out using these methods:
1. Market research
2. Speculative

Market Research

This takes time and to do it well and it also takes money. I briefly cover paid market research but if you want more advice on paid market research there will be a link in the bibliography at the end.

Surveys

Surveys are a great way find out who might like your solution, you can also ask them if they would pay for the solution and even how much they would pay. Google forms is a great free way to conduct a survey.

Statista

This is a great website finding out a whole bunch of info on your target audience. They have paid options too but they offer a lot of free info. They're basically people who have done a LOT of surveys and compiled it for you to buy. Pro tip; If you are a student or you know someone in full time education the price is greatly reduced.

Free events

Just like we discussed in the 12 Core captaincies, you can offer people your solution for free. Or at least part of it if you're getting good. Make sure you get feedback from everyone who attends.

Social Media

Social Media is a great way to test the waters on a product. I personally built an Instagram of 10,000 followers before I decided to do this. One of the great myths about selling online is that you need to already have the solution to see if it will sell. That's completely not true, otherwise you wouldn't be reading this book right now.

If you have a bit of a budget you can pay for Facebook ads, because Facebook knows everyone in its audience, they can tell you what kinds of people liked or looked at your ad.

The Avatar

This is a model of your ideal customer. Your ideal customer is going to be a composite of the 3 reasons, in that they are; 1) a person who will need it, 2) a person who is able to afford it, and 3) a person who likes it.

To do this, we need to figure out a few things about our audience.

1. What are they like?
2. How much do they have?
3. How much they know about the topic?

I fit the model perfectly for a program called WildFit (getwildfit.com).

I'm serious about weight-loss because I used to be 565lbs but I can't get rid of this last bit, I have more than $1500 in savings and I'm at an intermediate to advanced level of health understanding.

This means I would need it, I can afford it and if I take the course, I won't be left thinking

"I could have just found all this out on YouTube"
Or:
"I knew all this before I the course".

Ideally you'd want to know a lot more about your Avatar than this. But it's a great start. If you know this, you can start marketing to people.

Facebook Ads

This one of the best market research tools out there. Because everyone who uses Facebook has their age, current city and has already liked pages and that can give us an insight to the kinds of people that liked our ad and will probably like our product.

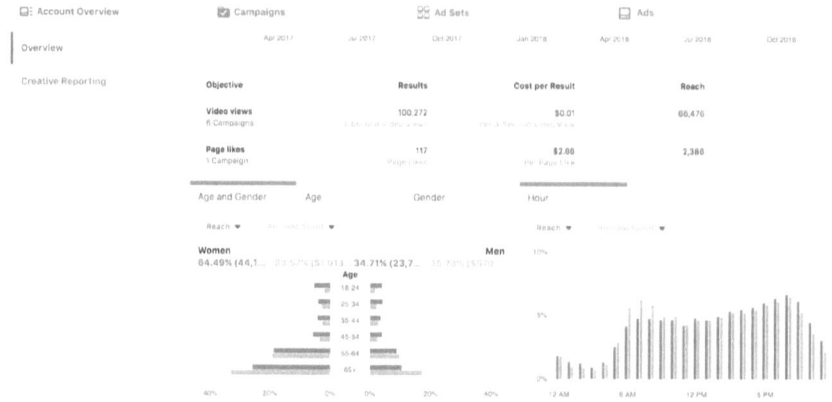

This output from a Facebook ad campaign shows us, how many people liked one of products, it shows us what percentage were men and what percentage were women. It even showed us what time of day people liked it most!

Market size

Now we know what our potential audience looks like, it's time to figure out how many of them there are.

Every single marketplace, whether it's digital or your local fruit market hast to draw a big enough crowed. Would you sell your fruit in a market if only 10 people turned up?

Fortunately Facebook has a handy tool for this too. If you go to create any ad in Facebook it will ask you to define your audience. If you leave it blank just market to everyone in the above example it will cost more and you'll get fewer results but Facebook will tell you what your Avatar looks like.

But when you know what your Avatar looks like you can just go ahead and program that into Facebook, the next time around.

If you go to:
https://www.facebook.com/adsmanager/creation
You will see a section that says Audience, it should look something like this:

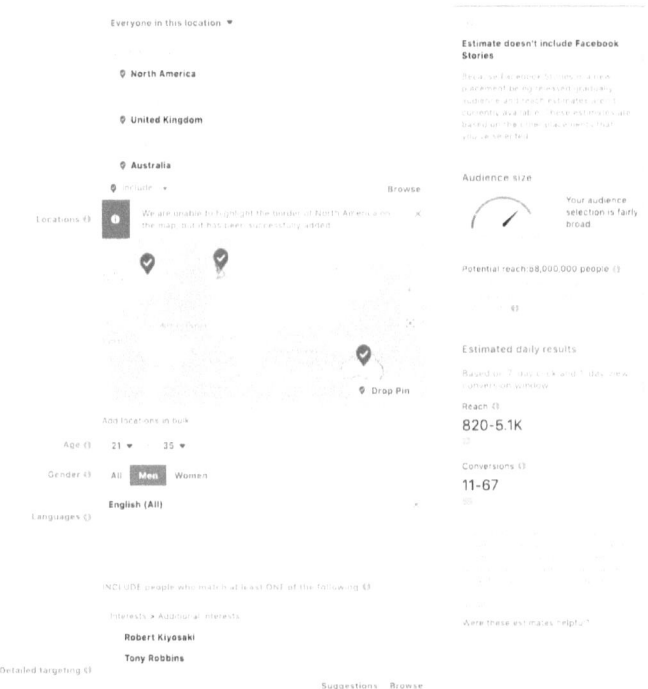

My Facebook Avatar

When I did my market research Facebook showed me I appealed to 63% males and 37% women. Does that mean I don't advertise to women? Hell no, but it does mean that 63% of my ad spend goes on men between the ages of 21 and 35 in the 5 major English speaking countries.

I also find that people who like Robert Kiyosaki and Tony Robbins also tend to like my solutions too. Maybe that's because they appeal to men who want to reinvent themselves or maybe because coaching with them is just out of their price range. It could be many reasons but I've found that seems to work.

So every time I create a new Facebook ad I input these values and Facebook only shows this ad to people who fall into that category.

But more importantly Facebook tells me there are 58,000,000 people in my marketplace. If there isn't at least 500,000 people in your market place it may not be worth serving that audience, depending on the signal to noise ratio.

Market share

Market share is difficult to calculate accurately. It's the number of other people that are also looking to reach that same audience (You didn't think all 58,000,000 of them were going to buy from me now, did you 🙂) and the percentage of that pie you share with them.

Google keyword planner is a great start. The keyword planner helps people looking to increase their organic Search Engine Optimisation (SEO) by telling them how popular a key world is and how in demand it. Signal to noise ratio.

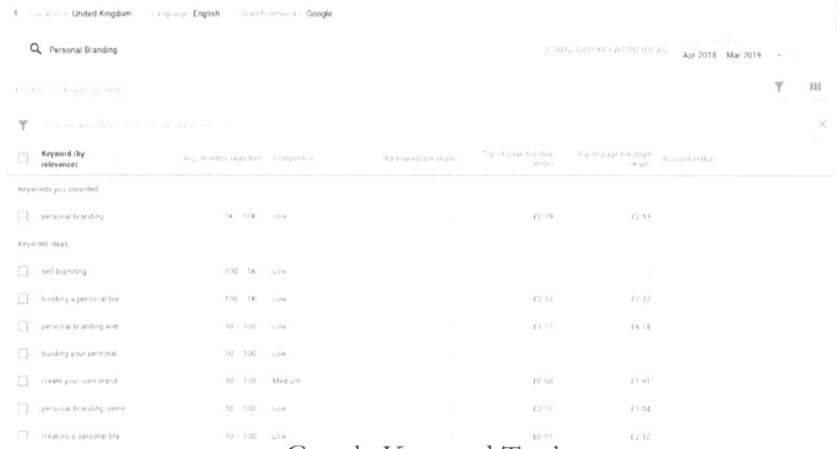

Google Keyword Tool

As you can see, the keyword planner tool shows us that personal branding has between 1000 and 10,000 people searching for it every month. It tells us that the competition in the UK is low and it suggests and AdWords spend of £2.55 (GBP) per click.

To me this shows that (in the UK at least), personal branding is something that people are looking for, but there isn't a lot of people trying to reach customers in this niche.

That's great news for me. But it's not bad if there are people in your industry already. Globally there are a lot of people teaching personal branding, but I bring my own experience and charm which helps me get my market share.

Of all the people out there teaching people personal branding, not many of them are doing it well and of the ones that are doing it well, they have their own unique style that appeals to some of the people but not all of them. Their price points are higher of lower than mine and so, some people will think they're too high and opt for me, some people will think they're too low and probably don't offer enough value and will opt for me.

You don't have to be the best, you have to be the right person. Your personal teaching style, the specific content you teach will appeal to a certain type of person at a certain stage in their journey. This process will help you figure who you're competing with.

There are at least 5 really big players in the personal branding industry that I know of. But you chose to buy this book. That means a percentage of the people who are looking for personal branding tips consult me.

The more people I work with, the more people who love my content the more my percentage of that market goes up (which reminds me, if you like this book please give it a review on Amazon, like it on Facebook, follow my Instagram and all that good stuff, thank you) and the more my brand grows.

The same is true for your brand, you might not have a huge market share right now, but once people experience your personal take on the topic and experience your amazing solution, they will tell their friends and your percentage of that pie will grow.

For now it's enough just to check what competition you have, who are the major players? What are they doing differently? What can you learn from them? How can you do it differently?

Summery

If want to provide a solution to people you have to know who they are. You have to know if they're a perfect fit for your solution. Selling someone something they don't want or need is unethical and they will likely want their money back.

Doing the research on exactly what kind of person would buy your solution is vital to your branding and improving your solution.

Key Takeaways

1. To sell a solution you have to know who will buy it
2. Make sure they need/can afford/want it
3. Use tools like Facebook and Statista to define your Avatar

10 creating content

This is my favourite section, I can talk about this section all day long. This is what I'm good at. I love solving people's problems. I especially love passing on the benefit of my experience.

You have done something in your journey to get where you are today. You've learned things, maybe not recently. Maybe for you to get where you are now it's taken years of realisations, setbacks, mindset shifts and generally becoming the person you are today, to build this new understanding of you profession.

Every goal has a journey to that goal and every journey has a story. This is your time to shine. Tell people about the dark days, don't make them depressed but people need to see that you went through this journey, they have to follow in your footsteps even if it's only while going through your solution.

Your goal as a solution provider is to take someone from where you were then, to where you are now.

The good thing about the internet is, it has allowed us to provide that solution to people over and over again, all over the world.

In the past, you could provide your solution to the people in your town, maybe even the next town across, or maybe you went to the city too, but sooner or later you would run out of people to sell the solution to.

The internet has opened you up to the world, so your solution can now be offered has to people all over the globe now. Your market place is no longer limited to just the people that can travel to it.

Let's start by talking about the types of content:
1. Blog
2. Email
3. PDFs
4. MP3s
5. Videos
6. Courses
7. Group coaching
8. Personal coaching
9. Ongoing content
10. Products as a Service (PaaS)

Blog

Having a blog today is easier than it's ever been. WordPress.com will fix you up with a free blog and you can get started today.

If you want to be a little bit more involved, you can download and install your own blog on your own hosting.

Be sure to check out my blog post on this for more: http://jamesvince.co/blog/setting-up-your-own-wordpress-2019

Or you could take a leaf out of my book and have someone build you a custom website and blog. Either way making a blog these is getting easier and easier and is usually always possible to do for free.

Why Blog?

There are 4 parts to a business:
1. Outreach (also called marketing)
2. Landing (sales presentation)
3. Sales (the actual sales process)
4. Loyalty (repeat custom and fan base)

A blog is one of the best forms of outreach, not only does it build authority and help you add value before they've even met you, it also builds good Search Engine Optimisation (SEO) which leads to free traffic (people visiting to your site).

Building a blog can be a create way to start content creation. I know many people who have written blogs for 2–3 years and then packaged it up into a book or a course and sold that.

Having a blog is a great way to get started in any industry. It can act as a journal while your still making mistakes you and who knows, in no time at all that blog could turn into your main solution.

Examples of great blog content ideas:
1. Start here (explain to first time visitors why they should stay)
2. Solve a common problem no one else is talking about
3. Share your story
4. Share your setbacks
5. Latest news and your opinion on it

Email

This is the glue that holds it all together. Email helps you keep the prospect interested as they move down the line of buying your solution. But it can also be used to automate the process, I talk more about this in chapter 12.

Examples of great email content ideas:
- Thank you and greeting messages
- Delivering PDFs and other content
- Links to your latest blog post
- Special limited time offers
- Introduction the next stage in the solution

PDFs

This a great way to add value at any stage of sales process. But it's usually used in the email gate stage.

In Chapter 12, I talk in detail about something the email gate. This is when you offer someone something for free (usually a PDF), in exchange for them giving you their contact details.

So I guess it's not really free. But offering someone value, in the form of a PDF is a great way to start the relationship.

PDFs also make great supplementary material. Sometimes you just can't explain everything you need to in a video or MP3, you need a little extra visual help. After all, a picture says a thousand words.

Sometime you might need audience participation, you might need them to write stuff down in a way that will help them understand. Using things like tables and forms for them to fill out can help guide them in the direction and keep them on track for the solution.

Examples of great PDF content ideas:
1. Infographics (help explain the problem/solution)
2. Top 7 mistakes people make when _____
3. Forms and Questionnaires
4. Visual things like diagrams and charts
5. Feedback forms (PDFs can be made editable)

MP3s

This is a great way to up sell someone who is ready to buy. Have you ever been in a grocery store, about to pay for your food and you see the candy bars lined up all along the checkout?

This is called an up sale. When you know someone wants to buy a part of your solution and you suggest another part of your solution. They will probably like the up sale product and it will add value to what they're already buying.

MP3s are also great to help explain off topic issues, if you have a course about doing business in Asia, the history of economics in China might not be directly relevant to your course, but you feel it could add some value and aid understanding of the main material.

Examples of great MP3 content ideas:
1. 7 steps to x (one per MP3)
2. Additional info not part of the main course
3. Anything that doesn't require video
4. Download the audio for the video
5. Thank people on the last MP3

Videos

If content is king, then videos are god. This is the number 1 way most people like to learn. This is one of the main reasons YouTube is so successful.

People are monkey see monkey do creatures, if we see something were are more likely to learn from it than reading or just hearing.

Videos help form the core of a course. In fact I took a course the other week and it was all text.

I asked for my money back immediately, not because the value of the content was low, but I have dyslexia, it would have taken me months to go through that content and probably a few more times over and fully understand it.

Video is a great time saver and it shows the person you respect their time. One of the worst things you can do to your users, is disable the controls on the video. Don't do this, let them know how long it'll be and let them pause it so they can come back to it later.

You ever been watching a video (probably on a sales page) and there's no pause button or length of time displayed on the video? They do that so you lose track in their 1 hours and 55 minute sales video. I respect your time, which is why when you hit on of my videos it's usually about 7 minutes long, even if it's a longer video you can always pause and see how long is left.

Don't ever let people download your videos, if you can, use Wistia to host your videos as they do some fancy tech magic to hide your video files. Your video files are the core of your solution, if they leak your solution will devalue fast.

Tai Lopez has some really great high value content, but unfortunately people have made it available on sharing sites. You don't want this to happen to you.

If it does it probably means you're doing something right, but it also means you need to improve your solution.

Examples of great video content ideas:
1. The main part of your course
2. Welcome, sales, up sell and solution presentation pages
3. YouTube (7 ways I tried to x)
4. Repurposed content (when you put the same content everywhere)
5. PDFs get given for free in email gates, but how many actually get read? Not many I imagine, maybe switch it up with a video or two as a thank you for signing up.

Courses

This is a big part of the solution, this is a grouping of all your content into one product. This is your story, this is the journey you took to go from 0 to 1 and this is what people pay for.

On the sales page you should list all of the types of content you'll get access to:

- 10 videos
- 5 MP3s
- 3 Infographics
- 2 PDFs
- 1 Group coaching session

This is called the value stack. Just like reading the contents of a book, your audience needs to know what they're getting for their money and if it isn't what they had in mind they won't reach the tipping point of value and they won't buy.

Group coaching

My personal favourite, the group coaching session. Remember aside from one-to-one coaching this is the most valuable thing you have to offer. It takes a bit more of your time than providing courses to people but it's worth it, you can set that higher price point and provide a lot more value.

For many people $300 an hour is crazy money, but now imagine 30 people are paying that just to hear you speak! That's $9000 for 1 hours work. So you better pack a lot of value into that hour.

The good thing about coaching sessions is you can usually sell them as package deal, I recommend once a week for 8 weeks.

I typically charge $2400 for my 8 week programs, this gives you 8 live webinars with me, 8 Q &A sessions, access the elite BRANDers Facebook group, an accountability partner assigned to you from either me or one of my staff and a free gift worth over $1000.

In those 1 hour webinars I know that I need to bring my A game, I need to bring all the value, they need to get just as much value as all my courses combined, they need to finish that program being able to apply the formula in their life from the very last day of the program.

Examples of great webinar software include:

- GoToWebinar – A little expensive at $69 a month but amazing features
- LiveStorm – Free option, great features full version is $99 a month
- EverWebinar - $597 one off fee
- Google Hangouts – Free limited control
- Zoom - Easy to use and free but no automation

Things to consider when choosing webinar software:

- Does it have webinar replays (for people who miss the session)

- Can you set it and forget it (Automation helps you just turn up to your programmed schedule and perform)
- Email and SMS reminders
- Chat feature, mute and kick functions

Personal Coaching

This is by far the most time consuming of all the solutions you can provide. On the flipside it's also the most lucrative.

Your time is valuable, your time is meant to be spent with your loved ones, on a beach, sipping cocktails (or something like that). So when someone wants to take you away from that you need some compensation.

This option is not recommended to people just starting out, but there's no reason why you shouldn't have this in the back of your mind. If you're not there yet, that's ok, start thinking of times where you really added value, times when you really changed someone's life. This will form your toolkit for when you start to offer personal coaching.

Personal coaching is hard to sell, there's no real defined learning. You can offer basic tuition to get people on the same page, they're gonna want something a bit more, well… personal.

At this level you must have experienced so many scenarios, and helped so many people that it comes as second nature to you to solve these kinds of problems. It's possible you might encounter the same problem in your personal coaching that you have in your group coaching, it's possible they have a generic problem, but don't count on it. People pay you good money at this stage to solve their bespoke problems. One size does not fit all here.

Personal coaching can be done in a group, it's just in person and more specific to them. I have trained small teams of people form the same company and my Bali retreats will train a group of 10 people who have never met each other before.

The one thing you have to remember at this stage is, you can sell them on the known results, but they have to leave with some unknown results.

This means you have to show to them that they will get some of their big problems solved, even if you don't know what they are yet.

This is a tough sell. I will solve your problem, even though I don't know what it is. But you're creative, you've been doing this for a while now and you're an expert. That's why they pay you the big bucks.

Ongoing Content

I have clients that pay me monthly, every month with no fixed outcome promised, they just have access to my Voxer account whenever they need it.

Voxer is a messaging app that allows you to send voice messages. A bit like WhatsApp or Line but without text. I know it's weird But it allows them message me any time day or night with a 7 second voice clip asking for my help with their branding issues.

This service is provided ongoing and to be a part of this service you have to pay a monthly retainer. If you provide any service that doesn't have an end date, it's ongoing content.

Product as a Service

If you have taken more than 2 of my courses, you will no doubt know that I offer access to all of my courses for one monthly fee. This is what we call a Product as a Service. It's any product that you restrict access to base on time.

When you buy one of my courses you're getting access to them based on content, you get limited access to the content, forever. But when you upgrade to unlimited access all of the content is available to you, I just restrict access to it for a 30 day periods instead of by course.

Any product you sell people access to base on time can be considered a PaaS.

Examples of popular PaaS include:

- Netflix
- YouTube Premium
- Spotify
- Shopify
- Hulu
- Diamond Dallas Page Yoga
- James Vince Unlimited

Ultimately any content you provide has to from your experience. You might have read about it before in a book or seen it on video, but you know what you know because of what you've learned and done:

1. Primary sources
2. Secondary sources

Anything you've done and had setbacks in, is considered a primary source anything you've read in books or gained in courses is considered secondary sources of content.

Secondary sources are not bad, but if it's iconic or known content you have to (where possible) do your best to site sources for your inspiration. I have done my best in the bibliography section below show credit to sources of information I gained from other people.

If you're providing coaching that shouldn't be a problem because it's verbal, but anything like a book, your blog or any written content it's best to site sources where you can.

Depreciation of value

Today the solution you have created has value. You've put a lot of time and effort into it and no one has compiled it and delivered it in the way that you intend to before.

The more you provide the content to people, the more people who are exposed to your solution, the more people that will know this. Robert Kiyosaki once said "Your house is not an asset it's a liability unless it brings you cashflow" and today it's the moto of almost every new YouTuber on the topic of money. It's not fair, but it's common knowledge now. His solution that was once making him millions, is now being used as free outreach material for other people.

Just like any asset, your solution will degrade over time, someone may leak it on file sharing websites, someone might copy you or you may just sell it to so many people in your niche that they all know the solution now.

Either way you have to be prepared for the fact that your solution will lose value and one day have no value. That's just how it is. So it's our job to contently keep improving the solutions we provide.

In 2018 I purchased of the "new and improved Tai Lopez's Social Media Marketing agency" course.

The number one tip in the Instagram section of the course is to take advantage of feature Instagram no longer supports.

Also the main tool they suggest to use for getting info on your competitors, ink361.com. Which is no longer up and running.

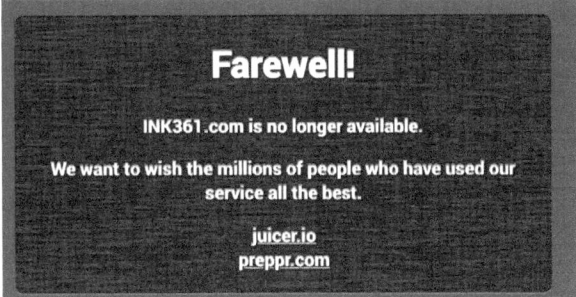

An update to the course might suggest that they use juicer.io or preppr.com.

So make sure your content is evergreen, that means it doesn't change a lot, the basics of business, doesn't change a whole lot, Facebook's user interface, changes all the time. Evergreen content.

Summery

There are many different types of content that you can use to form solutions that will provide value to your customers and help you live the life you want.

Using them add value to a solution helps the customer feel like it was a fair trade for their money.

Remember a trade only occurs when both people feel they have enough or more value they parted with.

If you're offered a Snickers bar for $60 you might feel the value just isn't worth it, because you know you can get a Snickers bar for under $3.

Key Takeaways
- Content is king
- Solutions have to solve a problem
- Different types of content can make different solutions

11 Branding the Solution

This is a vital part of the branding process.
Having a solution is great!
But if you don't know how to communicate and deliver that solution,
you may as well not have one.

Building an image that is approachable, and understandable is crucial.
Ralph Waldo Emerson taught that genius often seems so obvious
when it's spelled out by smart people. That's because the real genius
is making a solution digestible.

> *"If you can't explain it simply, you don't understand it well enough."*

> Albert Einstein

Making something look sexy and delivering to them in a way people
can consume, without getting information overload is crucial. If you
don't have a simple S.Y.S.T.E.M the person consuming your content
will get confused and wonder off.

S – Saving
Y – You
S – Stress
T – Time
E – Energy
M – Money

Most people, when they first start out, build a website, maybe they do
a little blogging, hope for some organic Search Engine Optimisation
but they don't have a real strategy, they throw themselves into
content, and then they throw that content down people's mouths
until they choke or buy.

Sure that will get you sales, but it doesn't get you respect, and it's
hard work too. You have to throw lots of money, time and energy at
it to see minimal return.

Wouldn't you rather have a well thought out strategy that attracts the right kinds of customers, who'd be happy to buy your content and what's more share it with their friends?

When Sean Parker invited Napster, back in 1999, the music industry was surprised. The music industry has so many pieces to the pie. At every level there's someone trying to take a cut.

Not least the record labels. They make the biggest coin in this chain. But for the artists, this showed people wanted to buy and share their content with their friends. What could be more of a sign you've made it than people sharing your content with their friends?

Note that I don't condone giving people's content away something for free. Especially when people put hours, days, months even years of their life into it. But the fact that people want to talk about and show your solution to their friends is great. It's a sign your content is "remarkable". The definition of remarkable is:

"Worthy of remarking about"

If people are talking about your content that means you're in high demand, it means they're doing 90% of the work for you.

 Do you know how much it would cost you to pay thousands, if not millions of people to be passionate about your content and tell people about it?
Just ask anyone who works in Network Marketing lol.

The point is your goal here is to build fans, brand ambassadors, early adaptors and innovators, whatever you call them, they're your tribe.

The vide you put out, determines the tribe you bring in.

This is why you have to make sure that the way you and your solutions come across speaks to the exact people that need it. This is why we need to craft the message we send out, specifically for the product or service we are trying to sell. We need a strategy that inspires people to go down a path to your product.

But we can't just say "Hey this is my awesome $1999 product come and get it". We need to build trust in the people we inspire, we need to build commitment to buy and then we need to build loyalty, so they will keep coming back to us.

Apple computers cost on average which is 3 times more than their windows equivalent, but 9/10 people will buy an apple computer over a Windows computer.

Luis Vuitton bags cost 10 times more than your average high street bag, but the people that buy LV products, seem to be buying them like a cop buys donuts.

Why is this?

Because they are part of the brand story.

When you buy a pair of Ray Ban sunglasses, it connects you to Goose and Maverick from Top Gun (if you're old enough to remember that), or it just shows the world you buy high quality well-made Italian designer products and it shows people you stand with this brand. Either way it sends a message that you stand with this brand.

Why do we stand with a brand?

We stand with a brand because they've never let us down before, we stand with a brand because they represent our values, because they're cool, because we gain from being associated with that brand.

What does this brand day about me?

I don't buy from Primark in the UK, because they employ slaves in developing countries and when their building collapses and kills most of the people inside, their first concern is covering up the story.

But I will buy Nike Jordan's (who probably do the same) because it makes me feel good when I'm wearing super cool shoes that people compliment me on. Is it hypocritical, hell yeah, am I being slightly insensate here? You betcha, but that's our association with brands. We stand by brands we feel make us cooler.

What do you stand for?

When people by your products and services, will they know what they are signing up for? Why will they stand with your brand?

When people buy from you, they have to instantly know;

"This is James Vince and he creates freedom in people's lives by helping them create micro income streams and growing them".

Be willing to be extreme

Whatever your reason for standing by a brand, it's probably extreme. How many people stand behind LL. Bean? I mean no offense to them, they're probably a great brand but they don't inspire hardcore fandom in most of us.

When was the last time you heard someone say "Yeah Colgate till I die man!".

Loyalty doesn't come from being agreeable, loyalty comes from standing your ground, being willing to stand out and be different. The most inspirational leaders of all time had extreme views (for their time):

- Martin Luther King
- Mahatma Gandhi
- Tenzin Gyatso (Given name for the Dalai Lama)
- Rosa Parks
- Anne Frank
- Malcom X
- John Lennon
- Notorious B.I.G
- Mother Teresa

All of these people stood for something so incredibly radical in their time that some of them were killed for those views.

I'm not saying you have to challenge the very foundations of civil rights to the point where someone wants you dead. But I am saying you need to have conviction in what you stand for and be willing to publicly acknowledge that this is what you stand for.

Mark Zuckerberg was once famously quoted for saying:

"You can't get to a billion friends without first making enemies"

You will encounter negative feedback, that's what happens when you stand for something. But I can guarantee you something, you will never be successful if you don't stand for something.

Delivering Consumable Content

Making sure your customers can understand you solution is one of the key factors that give it value (along with how much are other people charging for the same solution and how valuable is it to the customer).

Remember your job is to leave the customer feeling like they got some value from going through this solution.

If you buy a $5000 course on advanced partial physics you're not gonna get a lot out it unless you:

1) Have the foundational knowledge understand it
2) Can relate to the course material and instructor

If you can't relate to the instructor or they're not likeable it can be really hard to listen to the rest of the video. How many times have you been on YouTube and the person leading the talk has a strange accent that's hard to hear, or they speak in a boring monotone voice? If you don't have a good video presence that's ok, you can talk and just show a presentation or a video of someone performing the task with your commentary but I highly recommend you do what you can to improve your onscreen persona and your voice patterns.

If this is something you have trouble with, you should check out the YouTube channel Charisma On Command

If you really can't be on the camera at all then you should hire someone to do it on freelancing sites although it does take something away from the experience. But at least you're doing something. I n the meantime check out the above channel and improve your on-screen charisma.

Break it down

Is it just me that thinks of this guy when I hear break it down?

Small is digestible

If you had to eat 4 huge birthday cakes in 1 hour could you? For some of us the answer is yes but realistically most people couldn't. But if I said you had to eat a small piece of birthday cake every day for the next year, apart from being board, you probably could.

Just like in discussed in the chapter on the Minimum Viable Solution, you should break it down into 7 or 8 segments showing each stage of the evolution you have to go through to get the results you want.

Remember people are paying to understand the solution not memorise it.

If it's a big problem it may complex solution and it's your job to make that solution digestible. If you know your topic well and you make the most complex problems seem easy to solve, you will be making money for a very long time.

The power of color

When you put any brand together, one of the first things you have to think about is color. A brand is a visual que that helps indicate or remind you of the experience you'll have with the solution.

If you're solution ends with them on a beach somewhere, then you're brand needs to trigger feelings of what it's like to be on a beach. If your solution is weight-loss, your brand needs to trigger the thoughts and emotions of weight-loss.

In the chapter "Who is it all for", we looked at who might actually want to buy your solution. What kind of person are they and what message do they get from our brand.

This is an amazing image that helps us understand what colors mean to us and the kind of people we attract when you use them.

Gray shows calm and balance, Green being peaceful and healthy, Blue shows trust and strength, Purple is the color of wisdom and creativity, Red suggests you're exciting, brave and willing to take risks, Orange suggests you're gonna have a fun time and finally Yellow implies things are going to get better.

Your brand should have no more than 3 colors, a primary, a background and a highlight. If you want to be more experimental that's great, but consult someone like myself before releasing a colorful brand into the world, this can backfire or it can be amazing, if done well.

As the picture shows, companies like McDonald's and Subway are trying to appeal to people who need a little optimism. Their market is people looking for something better than they already have.

Although you might not actually feel that when you experience their solution, that's what they want you to feel.

Brand Consistency

This is huge, if you don't actually provide the experience that your brand suggests you do, people will be disappointed with their experience while using your solution.

How many times have you gone into a store expecting to get exactly what you needed, then after you feel a little bit cheated. That's called buyer's remorse.

That doesn't necessarily mean they conned you, but it could mean you weren't right for their product. Either way, there was a problem with the message they send out.

The vibe you put out determines the tribe you bring in.

Take some time to think about exactly what you want your customers should to feel when they experience your solution. Look back at your customer avatar and ask yourself, what do they want to see, what would make them think of the results of your solution.

The logo

People go backwards and forwards on this all the time. Do you need a logo?
My answer is ask Sir Richard Branson. The Virgin signature has become iconic, the Nike logo instantly forms an image of running shoes in your head. I'm not allowed to used it for copyright reasons, but imagine there was a Starbucks logo below. They removed the word Starbucks from their logo in 2011. How many of you would still instantly think Starbucks when you see it?

A logo is a powerful thing and make no mistake you need one. But just like Starbucks, you too can have changes to your logo, but you have to be careful, people often respect an upgrade in logo, but if you change your logo to often for no reason, especially before you've had the chance to make everyone aware of your brand you might get some kickback.

If your budget is low here is a list of really great online logo makers:
- https://hatchful.shopify.com/
- https://logojoy.com/logo-maker/
- https://www.renderforest.com/logo-maker

If you have a bit more in your budget I highly recommend Fivver.com, Freelancer.com and Guru.com to get yourself a seriously cool logo.

Theme design

I remember sitting back in my university hall, during a lecture on usability, by some famous guy in the industry, thinking "snoooooooorrrrre, when am I ever gonna use this?
I'll just make what I want and they can use it."

I should have been paying attention more. The only thing I remember from that whole semester was A/B testing is when you show users one design, analyse if they liked it or not, then do the same with another design and see which one gets more attention.

While that is valuable (actually probably the best thing to take away from usability to be fair), I didn't realise that A/B testing comes after the fact.

When building a web page there are some already pre-tested ideas that have been proven to work, so we don't wanna re-invent the wheel.

One proven thing is the design flow, just as in sales the design flow should follow 6 simple steps:

1. Show the results
2. Explain the problem
3. Make the problem relatable
4. Present the solution
5. Support the solution
6. Call to action

Show the results

To catch people's attention you need a big sign that says

"This is what having the solution looks like".

You'll notice on my website, JamesVince.co I have a big banner that shows me in exotic places all over the world helping people and on stage.

Well a picture says a thousand words right? So ideally the image should say that. If you're selling weight-loss products, a massive compilation of before and after photos should do the trick.

If you're selling the laptop lifestyle from Thailand then some pictures of you in a hammock drinking cocktails with your laptop on you lap should do just fine.

But whatever you put there, it needs to make them feel what it's like to have the solution.

Explain the problem

Have you ever had a word on the tip of your tongue but you just can't bring it out?

 Most people have, if you were selling Alpha Brain, a natural herbal supplement for increasing your brain power, then this is would be a great way to start it.

If they are experiencing the problem, and you describe the problem to them, it's gonna make them wake up and say

"HEY!, I have that problem".

Make the problem relatable

Sometimes this step is called exaggerate the problem, but I don't like to use this because it makes it sound manipulative. Showing someone that you know how they feel is a lot better than really pushing the buttons on their pain.

Either way they have to emotionally connect and feel that you understand what they're going through, you could give a specific example of what happened to you or a client (change the names of your clients) but either way they need to see the problem in action and they need to know that you get them.

Present the solution

This is where you introduce your course. maybe with a video, maybe just a few bullet points with icons, whatever that looks like for you, make sure you show them what your solution does.

Support the solution

This is the testimonials section. Ideally this would be a mixture of videos and images. Some people really wanna see movement, real life people and some people just don't have the time. They just wanna see real people getting real results fast.

You should have testimonials at this point. In the 12 Core competencies you should have done an event where people came for free. You would have taken their emails. Go back and ask them what they thought.

Call to action

This seems like a no brainer right? But you'd be surprised at just how many people don't ask people to buy their product. The best way to do this is with a video but on my page; jamesvince.co
I have this banner:

This is a clear indication I want them to do something. Notice a call to action doesn't have to be a buy button. We're not at that stage yet, we have to talk to people at the level there are at.
You wouldn't walk straight up to someone with you product in hand and say buy my tea! So neither should your website.

Templates

The great thing about living in the 21st century is many things have already been done for you. FOrtunatly theming websites is one of them.
There's a great website called ThemeForest.net with some of the best templates on the internet, for all the popular website management systems.
They even have templates for each step in the sales process. If you search for landing page or sales page, you'll get hundreds of great landing pages. If you search thank you pages, they have those too. If you search book sales page, guess what, they have that too. So defiantly head over to Theme Forest for some great templates.

Brand awareness

The goal of brand awareness is to help customers through the different stages of being aware of you and your solution.
The stages are:

1. Awareness of problem
2. Awareness of industry
3. Awareness of your brand
4. Awareness of your solution
5. Interest in your solution
6. Desired to have your solution
7. A customer of your solution
8. A loyal fan of your solution

Awareness of problem

Some people have a problem and don't even know they have it.
Did you ever have a pair of shoes that just got so worn out but you continued to where them?

In 2013 I had a pair of Reebok Classics, I'd wanted a pair since I was 10 years old, they were all the rage when I was in school.
I finally had disposable income and I just happened to pass a store that had them. So I bought them. To tell you the truth, they didn't quite live up to what I had imagined 20 years ago.

If I'm honest, I'm just super stubborn and wore those shoes day in day out for way longer than I should have. Because of pride.
I'd finally got the shoes of my childhood and they were super uncomfortable.
But did I let that stop me from wearing them clean through to my foot? No way!

I may have been aware deep inside that I needed a new pair of shoes but you couldn't tell me that at the time. If you came to me and said "looks like you need a new pair of shoes", I'd have said "actually these ones are doing me just fine, thanks".

The moment a prospect says to themselves
"you know, I think I need help with x"
That's when they become aware of the problem.

If you sell coaching, the person has to admit they're life isn't exactly where they want it to be, and that's a tough pill to swallow.

Awareness of the industry

If you've ever had a complicated problem, you might not be aware that someone is selling a solution to it. Most balding men think that the solutions to male pattern baldness are to:

1. Hide you head with a hat
2. Shave all of your hair off
3. Wear a wig or toupee
4. Grow the hair that you do have ridiculously long and fold it back over the bald spot (this one is amazing!)

Most people don't know that there are scientific experts out there that can actually stimulate dying hair and even recreate new ones, it's truly incredible.

If someone is not aware of your solution the language you use might look something like this:

"Did you know there are new scientific break throughs in the field of Trichology (hair science) that allows us to completely regrow dying and even dead hair?"

This market has been saturated with scams for so long that simply presenting them with yet another product that may or may not work for them, isn't going to cut it (pun intended).

They don't think there is a solution.
At this stage, it's your job to show them that there is.

Awareness of brand

You're probably aware of coffee. It's a solutions that's been around for about 400 years now, but are you aware of Kalsada?

Chances are, if you've never been to Manila in the Philippines you probably won't have heard of them.

In early 2017 I was asked to sell coffee for a company called Organo. They sell coffee infused with a special Japanese herb that helps Japanese people live so long.

Everyone who sells Organo makes people try the coffee before they tell you anything about the company.

Most coffee drinkers have a brand, be it Starbucks, Maxwell house, Nescafé, or some other brand I've not heard of.

If you don't introduce the brand and why you should buy from this brand you may find yourself fighting an uphill battle against their long loved brand.

You must make people aware of your brand and what it stands for before you introduce to your solution.

"Hi my name is James and I help people transform their lives by learning how to add extra income streams".

Or.

"Hi my name is James and I sell a course on how to make more money."

Which would you prefer on your first meeting with me?

Awareness of your solution

Once someone is fully aware of who you are, they are more willing to listen to what you have to say.

You can talk to them like an old friend at this point.

"Hey Dave, how've you been? By the way I've been thinking about your problem with x, you know I offer a training program that helps people deal with exactly that".

Make sure they're aware of what you sell but make sure to leave a little mystery at this stage, so they will want to know more.

Interest in your solution

Once someone is interested in your solution you can tell them a little more about it, the benefits and the features.

But most people don't know the difference between a benefit and a feature.

People don't by a Ferrari because it has a V8 engine, most people buy a Ferrari because how it makes them feel.

Yes the V8 engine is what creates the feeling, but that's not what sells it.

What sells the car is the experience.

Ever wonder why people let you drive around in the car for free, for sometimes half a day?

Here's a list of different ways to describe a solution :

Feature	Benefit
V8 Engine	Makes people notice you
3 pdfs, 13 videos, 9 mp3s & 2 .txt	Increased social interaction
5 days in Bali	Improve your life while relaxing
150 pages	Life changing
45 inches	The perfect gold swing
3 sessions	A new life
Membership to a Facebook group	A support network
2 sticks of butter	Tastes like heaven
400 foot swimming pool	Kids occupied all day

I could go on but I think you get the idea.
This is how you form your value stack.

A value stack is the list of features and/or benefits that help create what we call the lollapalooza effect, a term created by Charlie Munger, that means the tipping point where someone says to themselves

"Actually, yes, I'm gonna buy this, right now!".

A customer of your solution

Well done, you made something people would like enough to buy.
But the story doesn't have to end there.
You can still provide them value and vice versa.

The next step is to turn them into your loyal fans.

We do this by getting feedback so we can serve them better. Ask them, what did you think about the solution. It's not just in training we have to evaluate.
Like I mentioned before, a solution devalues over time. The only way we can find out how to calculate the value that your solution still has is by asking people. Did it meet your expectations?
If not what can I do about it? What was missing from solution that you hoped you'd get from it? How can I provide you with more value?

Some people just aren't right for you and that's ok.
Give their money back and go about your business serving other people.

But never pass up an opportunity to learn from your setbacks.

If they loved it, then even better you need to show this person some love. Give them some more free stuff they might like. This is the make or break stage, they will either fall completely in love with you at this stage or be like "yeah that person was kinda cool".

You want them to fall in love with you. So get them to join the on-going support Facebook group if they haven't. Get them to like the page, check you out on YouTube and Instagram, this is the time to get them involved.

Don't make another ask from them until you have attempted to convert them into a fan.

The loyal fan of your solution

You did it! This is the goal of any business, to make fans!
Don't believe me? Take it from McDonald's.

The average sale for a first time customer in McDonalds is $1.38
McDonald's ad spend per customer is $2.57

That means if someone comes in and only buys one time, they lose money. Obviously McDonald's is doing pretty well so we can safely assume most of their customers come back at least once.

A loyal fan is the most valuable customer a business can have. That means if you want to up sell them (offer another product at the point of sale) they're more likely to take it. That means they will wear a T-shirt with your logo on and proudly tell people about you.

Did you ever see someone with a Honda Tattoo?

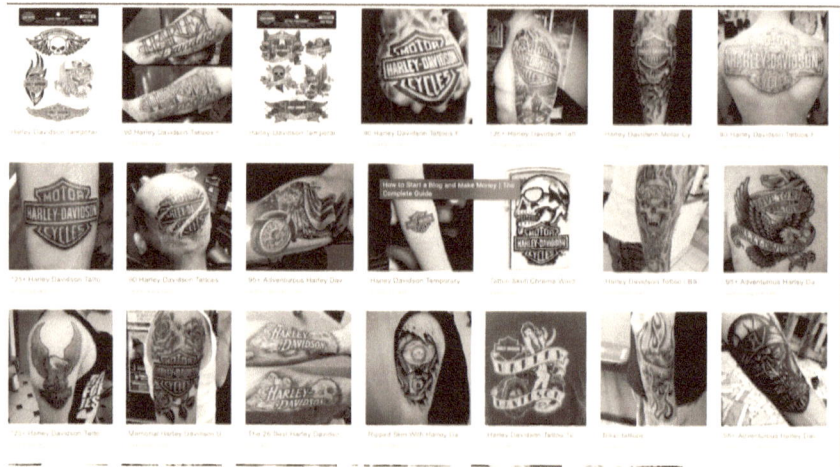

Yeah me neither.

This is the reason we're in business. We're not in business to make everyone kinda happy. We're in business to make some people want tattoos of our brands on their bodies!

The riches are in the niches

This saying only really works in the US where niches has a harsh sound like witches and rhymes with riches, in the UK is just sounds like the riches are in the neeshes.

Anyway…

Just like Vespa "isn't for everyone", nether are you and nor do you want to be. Being or everyone is boring. Corn Flakes is for everyone, Rice Pudding is for everybody, you want to be Cholula hot sauce. Not because you want to ruffle feathers but because that's who you are. Unless you're the most boring person in the world (which you're not because, everyone reading this book is awesome!), you have something special inside you, you have something that makes you different, and you need to let it shine.

The vibe you put out determines the tribe you bring in.

People like us do things like this

Lewis Hilsenteger is a YouTuber who has gained massive success because he opens electronic gadgets in his videos.

It's become popular these days to feel the joy that comes with opening consumer electronics. It's like receiving an xmas present every day.

His built up a following of nearly 15,000,000 people.

People like Lewis (his audience) unbox consumer electronics.

Summery

To make your solution pop you need to package it in just the right way.

Building an image around who you are and what you stand for is crucial. When people look at the Virgin logo they see excitement, adventure and fun. What's more, the experience with your solution has to match that feeling. It has to do what it says on the tin. If you're a full on adrenaline junkie, show it!
If not, may wanna stick to something more your pace.

People are attracted to what they think is cool. If you are what they think is cool, show them. Put out your vibe and you're sure to bring in a tribe just like you.

Key Takeaways

- To stand out you need to be different (you are different)
- To sell you have to show people why you're different
- People are at different stages of awareness of your solution
- Just like real life, you have to meet them where they're at
- Our goal as solution providers is build loyal tribes

12 AUTOMATING THE PROCESS

Using words like "Do you need high quality websites at low prices?" speaks to a prospect that outsources website production for other people. More importantly it speaks to people who want quantity not quality.

If you can make 5 websites a day and you value your time at $10 per hour then this might be for you. But we didn't get into this to earn less than we're earning at work, we need to refine what I call the customer voice.

Using your client Avatar we can find out about our ideal client. Age, gender, interests and so on. These tell you how to speak to your prospects and it also lets them know if they want to work with you.

The customer voice is the language you use to talk to your customers. You can buy in any language, but you have to sell in the language of the buyer. This means if your client is very political, starting the conversation off with why the current administration is causing your business to slow down, might be amazing, it might also be terribly offensive.

On the other hand if your client is Justin Bieber, knowing a lot about pop culture and wearing clothes that fit his age and social group is exactly the way he would want to be dealt with. If you know his slang and popular phases you'll get on like a house on fire. Remember you're there to help people and you can't help them if they don't like you.

Value stacks are the key selling points you know you can deliver on, in the exact way you say you can deliver. With creative services it's define exactly what you will get as a finished product, but you can use words that attract the right clients

We also need to know where in the buying process a prospect is. If you use phrases like:

"This revolutionary new product really does cure baldness, learn more" we know this is the first time they've heard of your product and it's the first time they've heard of you.

Using phrases "Magic grow, the product that makes your hair grow best" shows us they are aware of the brand, they're aware of what it does and you just want to tell them they you're the best at it.

The next stage is "You haven't bought Magic Grow yet? Make the change!" is talking to an audience that knows all about you but hasn't thought to by your product yet.

The final stage talks to the repeat customer "Did you like Magic grow? Get another box free if you refer a friend!". When we know where someone is in the cycle, we can start to build our value stack.

This process is known in the marketing business, as a sales funnel. Steps and procedures you take, then the prospect takes, then you take, then the prospect takes. It's a bit like playing chess, you try to think of the most likely move your opponent will do so you can counteract. Heres an example of the kind of sales funnel I use.

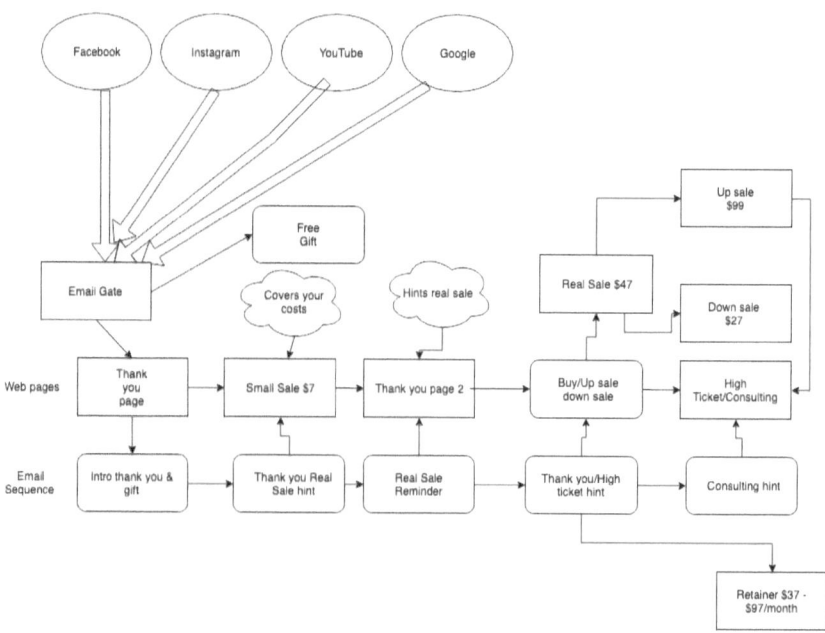

Stage One
Typically you start with some kind of social media, (YouTube, Instagram and Facebook are dominating at the time of writing), then your post, video or image will encourage them to get the free gift that sits behind the email gate.

Stage Two
The Email Gate is a page on your website that asks the prospect for some kind of contact details (usually email) so you can hint at them to buy. When they give us their email, they are sent to a thank you page which gives them their free gift (usually a PDF) and makes them aware of the of next stage, the small sale.

Almost 99.9% of people don't go straight from stage one to stage two, because they haven't built up enough trust in you yet. You haven't offered enough value to take from them.

For me this is 2 pdfs, "You are your brand: A guide to reinventing yourself" and the first chapter of this book along with the first half of a 13 mp3 series on Discovering Your purpose.

You get 7 for free and you have to pay for the other 6. You have to invest $7 for in my small sale, the rest of the MP3s. Almost everyone who goes through and listens to the first 6 feels compelled to buy the rest.

Not only do they provide so much value, but the second half completes the big picture. Also number 7 ends on a cliff hanger.

Stage Three

If they don't the small sale on the thank you page, or they just didn't see it because they were in a hurry, an email reminder will be sent to them, looking something like this:

> Dear [Prospect Name],
> Thank you for picking up a copy of [Your free gift name],
> I don't know if you had time to notice but I'm also offering my [small product name] for just $7! This product shows you exactly how you can [insert benefits here] and fully [list the results of your solution].
> One of the key principals I discuss in [product name] is:
> - [Insert small part of solution here]
>
> You're not gonna miss the rest: **get it NOW and start seeing results**!

If they click the link, it should take them to a page that offers them your small sale. This has to be more valuable than $7 because we want them to compelled to buy it. So the should get $50 or even $100 worth of value. Most people won't refuse something of that value.

For me it looks like the second half of the mp3 series they got for free in stage one. Allowing them to complete the set and get the full value.

If they don't click the link they will get another email, reminding them they missed out on my offer.

This message is set to go out to them every day for 7 days at the same time.

Stage Four
The thank you page for buying the full mp3 series introduces one of my courses called "Own Your Life". A $99 (USD) video series designed to help you reclaim your life and unlock your true potential. If they bought my $7 mp3 series they are more likely to

buy one of my courses than they would be going from stage one to stage two. But still the conversion rate at this stage is still low.

Your customers trust you enough to buy from you, but are they willing to step it up, did they get enough value from your initial free gift, the mp3 series and the emails you've sent them. They may pass up the offer. Or they may just not see it (again lol).

Same process again if they don't buy. They are sent the offer very day for 7 days again.

Stage Five

After purchasing "Own Your Life" I give them time to process their purchase. To go through the course and fully get the benefits of it.

After 2 weeks I send them an email inviting them to join my elite BRANDers coaching program.

Over 8 weeks they get 8 webinar sessions with myself, homework after each session, 2 x Q&A sessions, access to the elite BRANDers Facebook group and they're assigned an accountability partner.

If they complete "Own Your Life" they get a pop up in the learning system to congratulating them and introducing the next course, and the next and so on. They are also introduces to the elite BRANDers program at each stage too.

Stage Six

By the time someone has completed my elite BRANeDers program and a few of my courses, they're either one of my loyal fans or they want their money back (That's fine. I have a 100% guarantee policy). But at this point the ones that stay really love what I have to say, and I've provided them with real value.

For the most part they become loyal fans at this stage.

At this stage, they trust that what they buy from you, will be worth what they pay.

They will not only be ready to purchase you high ticket item in trust, but they will also be ready in development.

Sure you can take people on directly at this level, but if someone has followed you through the journey to reach this level of development it makes the experience loyal and meaningful.

For me, this my retreats. This year it's an all-expenses paid trip to Bali for a 5 day intensive training, in the stunning Hanging Gardens of Ubud.

The Bali retreat includes 3 parties, 2 poolside buffets a thick heavy workbook packed full of useful exercises and you're also assigned an accountability coach too, to help you stay on track and make sure you bring you're A game.

Maybe they're not ready for something this big, maybe they just love my courses and want access to all of them all the time. That's ok too. At this stage I send them the following email.

Hey [Customers name],

I saw that you've a couple of taken a couple of my courses.

You also indicated in the survey I sent you that you got a lot of value from them.

For people who really love my courses I offer unlimited access to all of my course for just $37 a month.

For this you get access to my entire library of courses, supplements and bonus videos.

Be sure to get access to:

- "Traveling expert" (Bonus Course)
- A BRAND new you
- Social Media Mastery

This offer is only available for the next 5 days.

Click here to get access to everything NOW!

The Final Stage

If you've made it this far it means

1) You really like what my solutions
2) You're ready to take your business to the next level

If this is you, then I probably spoke to you after one of my retreats about my consulting sessions. Maybe gave you my personal telephone number and asked you to call when you felt you're ready for it.

When you are, you'll arrange a meeting with your accountability coach to go over some of your biggest challenges in taking your expert business to the next level.

They will remind you that a coaching session with me costs $750 (USD) per hour over video chat or $1000 (USD) per hour plus transportation for in person sessions (as of writing).

I don't charge this much because I want to exploit people, I charge this much because I don't want to do consulting.

My time is valuable to me. Who I spend my time with personally is an important decision because that's less time I get to spend with the people I hold dear to me.

I also value the solutions I provide to my clients greatly. I can't provide the same solution to multiple people at this stage because they're all specific to the client.

So once that solution is given, there's pretty much no more value I can derive from it. It adds to my experience and helps me better serve other clients but that particular solution is gone. Absorbed into me and them.

Sales Funnels

The art and science of directing people through your solution, from the email gate to high ticket is known as sales funnels.

Probably the world's best known sales funnels expert is Russel Brunson. Author of Dot Com Secrets. He is also the person who coined the term funnel hacking.

Funnel hacking is improving the efficiency of your sales funnels by testing different options until you get it right.

Russel Brunson is also the inventor of Click Funnels, a tool for helping you create and modify your sales funnels in seconds. Not just conceptually but it will also make all of the webpages and email links for you. All you have to do is change the names of your products and services and Input your company information.

It's completely revolutionised the world of online marketing and without it, many people wouldn't be able to automate their sales funnels.

A sales funnel should have a traffic source; Facebook, YouTube or some kind of ad, a webpage with an email gate on it called a squeeze page and if they accept the email offer they are then sent emails of value, followed by emails to buy something.

Frank Kern, one of the best marketers of our times says that, if you want someone to buy from you, provide them with so much value before they buy that they will beg you to work with them.

Garry Vee went one step further and said you have to give 2:1.
This means for every stage of the solution you want to sell, you must give them 2 parts of the solution first.

The basic sales funnel looks like this:

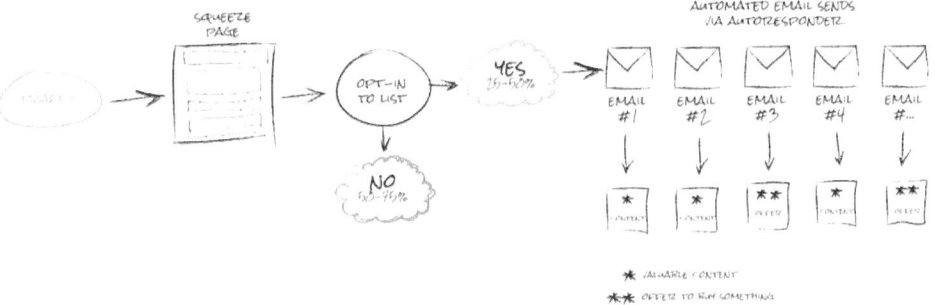

Example of a basic Sales Funnel

It is possible to build this sales funnel and many others without using Click Funnels. Click Funnels can run a little expensive for the first time income stream builder. So if you don't already have a good amount of cash saved up or invested in your new income stream, it's probably best to build your own.

Cruip.com has some really nice sales pages that you can download in exchange for your email gate info.

I have also built a couple of really nice squeeze pages you can download for free at:

www.JamesVince.co/resources/landing

Thank you pages

Thank you pages are not essential but make a big difference. Some people are impulsive and want to buy again. So you'll lose that percentage of people if you don't have a second offer for them. But perhaps more importantly, you gain a little respect with a thank you page.

It's also a great place to give out free gifts.

Email tools

As I mentioned before, email is the glue that holds all of this together, and sending emails that sell is an artform in and of itself. I wish I had scope in this book to write a whole chapter on how to write good copy. Maybe I'll write about it in a future book.

But for now let's look at the kind of email sequence you might get from me depending on which funnel you come in through.

The meet and thank email

Welcome [customer_name],

I'm so glad you have chosen to take your life to the next level and gain new income streams. Your copy of [email_gate_item] is on its way to your inbox as I type.

I wonder if you had chance to check out the free MP3 half series on [solution_name].

If you didn't, don't worry, I have the complete MP3 series available here.

Thank you so much for joining the BRANDers family, I'm sure you're gonna get a lot of value and growth from it.

Yours,

James Vince
JamesVince.co
Instagram: @james0vince
Facebook: FB.com/james0vince

This email not only thanks them for joining the BRANDers family but introduces the next stage of the funnel.

Notice I didn't say anything about the price. Having a price there may instantly disqualify the prospect. Give them time to get to know you and your offer more form the sales page.

Post-sale email

Hey [customer_name],

Thank you for purchasing my MP3 series on [solution_name], I'm sure you'll get a lot of value from it.
It details how I overcame [the_challenge_it_solves] and went on [get_x_result].

You may have seen on the thank you page there was an offer for my book [name_of_book]. This book is essential supporting material for the MP3 series as it takes it further and shows you exactly how you can [solution_of_the_book].

Normally this book retails for [price] on Amazon, but because you bought the MP3 series [solution_name] I want to off you the following discount code to get it at 50% off the RRP.
Your promo code is: [promo_code]
Thank you again for purchasing the MP3 series, until next time.

Yours,

James Vince
JamesVince.co
Instagram: @james0vince
Facebook: FB.com/james0vince

At this stay they're a customer. They have proven they will they like what you offer them and by offering them a discount, your providing even more value.

Remember the goal here is to add value. Take a long term view, this is building a relationship and you can't build a relationship without adding value.

This is an important stage in the buying process. The first purchase and how they feel about it, will determine how they move forward with the rest of your solution.

The no show email

In the next section I will talk about how we can know if prospect has bought our solution or not, but for now let's suppose they haven't.

Hi [prospect_name],

Thanks again for [downloading/buying] your [free] copy of [the_next_stage_of_the_soltuon].

I really hope you got a lot out of it.

I noticed that you didn't take advantage of the offer to get [the_next_stage_of_the_soltuon] for just [price].

It's really essential support material for the [the_previous_stage_of_the_soltuon].

It details how I overcame [the_problem_it_solves],
And helped me to:
1. Gain financial freedom
2. Travel the world
3. Spend more time with my loved ones

I'm pretty sure, you're not gonna want to miss this!

Yours,

James Vince
JamesVince.co
Instagram: @james0vince
Facebook: FB.com/james0vince

Thank them for their previous involvement. You respect their input and want to let them know. It reminds them of the value they're missing out on and encourages them to buy it if they missed out.

This email is sent to them once a day in the morning.

The apology email

The above email is usually sent to them 5 times before I offer them a promo code for a discount (where possible) on the 6th day. On the 7th day I send them an apology that looks like this.

Dear [prospect_name],

It pains me to say this, but I think my emails aren't providing you with value.

They're either going into your spam folder or you just don't like receiving them.

It's ok, I get it, I'm not for everyone and I'm really sorry to have taken your time and space in your inbox.

Could I ask that you do me one small favour though?
Please check out this questionnaire I made for people who don't get value from my content and let me know exactly what it is you didn't like about it?

JamesVince.co/forms/unsubscribe

It really helps me serve people better.

James Vince
JamesVince.co
Instagram: @james0vince
Facebook: FB.com/james0vince

At the end of the form they're offered the chance to unsubscribe from the emails and never here form me again.

If not they will receive the no show email will be sent once a week for as long as they remain on the list. You never know, one day they might see it and think

"Oh James Vince, I remember that guy, I should check in with him".

If you stop sending them messages while they're on the list you not only rob the chance to see it later, but you also miss out on sales.

Email Subjects

Email subjects are arguable more important than the content of the email. They decide whether or not the email even gets opened.

A couple of things to consider with titles:

- Is it relevant to the content?
- Does it give to little or too much away
- Does it feel like a robot made it
- Does it feel like a script

The best kind of email subjects are ones that encourage them to open the email. For example:

- Did you catch the game last night?
- How is this possible?
- There no way she could have…
- Over $400,000 in revenue in 3 months…
- John, you missed our meeting!
- Maria, don't miss out on…

The challenge here is not sounding too cheesy, it's super hard to come up with email subjects that encourage the customer to open, are relevant to the content of the email and don't sound super cheesy.

Fortunately the guys at CopyHackers have your back:

https://copyhackers.com/2012/08/writing-email-subject-lines-improve-open-rate/

These guys are the masters of writing emails that sell and they give away so much free advice and tips that it's almost impolite not to include their input in your emails.

Automation tools

The best way to get your business on autopilot is still with online automations tools. Having an auto-responder for your emails, having websites and sales pages that know who has bought what and when and ideally the whole thing could be automated.

Full Automation

If you have the budget for it, there really is no better solution to automating your business than Click Funnels. The master of funnels Russell Brunson has completely blown everyone out the park when it when it comes to automated sales funnels.

But there are some people who come close. If you're budget can't stretch to $97 a month out the gate then you might wanna consider these guys:

- Unbounce.com – A little cheaper at $79 a month
- LeadPages.net – Pricing starts from $25 a month
- InstaPage – Starts at $99 a month
- Builderall – A second rate Click Funnels from $9.99 a month

Full automation in one company has it's upsides and it's downsides. It means you have a single point of failure, if that site goes down, you whole funnel gets wiped out, not fun.

Email Tools

A great place to start is MailChimp. It's free connects to a whole bunch of different social media, shop tools and website managers. The back end is really to use and they make the process of templating and sending mail much easier than others. If your budget is low and you just need something simple until you learn about more complicated tools then this is perfect.

MailChimp is not without its flaws. Because it's used by a lot of spammy, porn, gambling and generally low quality companies. This gives it a low Sender Score. The Sender Score is ranking from 0-100 on how likely this is to be unwanted content. Basically if it's low, it's going in spam, it may get into their inbox depending on what level their email client is set to spam.

GetResponse

This is by far my favourite email tool probably the most powerful.

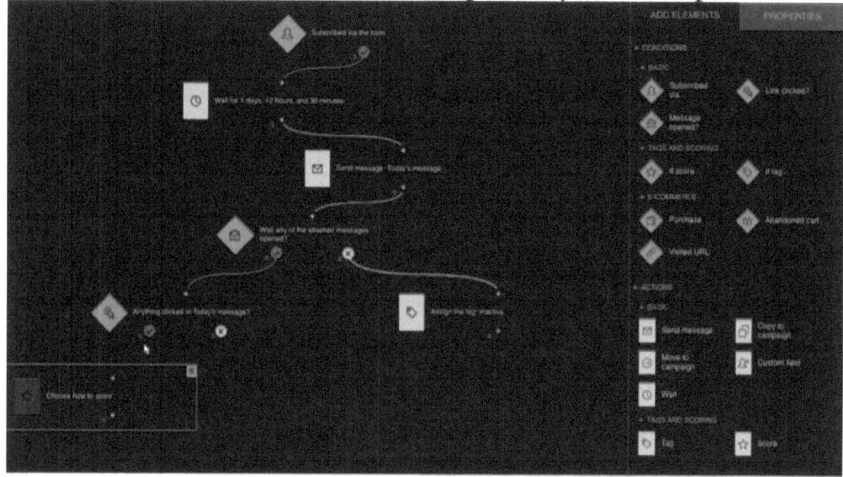

GetResponse Marketing Automation

This is most likely the most innovative tool available for email auto responders.

It's relatively simple to use you can hook it into your WordPress (through the OptimizePress Plugin), it's sequencing is incredible.

You can set a 2 day delay, you can set one email to go out for 3 days and then another then go back to the first and you can do it all from this handy drop and drag design interface.

If you've ever been sent an automated message from me, it came from GetRepsonse. I do have to point out that I get paid to promote GetResponse with affiliate links and they have sponsored some of my videos on YouTube.

To get a discount code for 2 months on me checkout:
JamesVince.co/codes/GetResponse

Don't let my being paid by them sway your opinion. I promote them because they genuinely are the best. I wouldn't use them if they weren't.

AWebber is a popular choice among bloggers. It was probably the first commercial email auto responder. You get a 30 day free trial, after that they start you on $19 a month. It's simple, just automatic email. Nothing special.

Drip

What review of auto responders would be complete without mentioning drip. They're the coolest new kid on the block. But their fees are a little high starting at $49 a month for less than 2500 people (it goes up to $122 if you have more).

You have to making some serious coin from your auto responder to warrant paying 6 times the average monthly price for basically the same service.

But young people love it because it's mostly used through their Applications Programming Interfaces (APIs).

It's technical but basically they can make it look like you're not using an email provider at all.

The API can let you (or more likely your web designer) create custom commands that perform tasks on their website through yours. That sounds complicated but in short it means no branding, no having to log into their website, you can build it all into your WordPress.

Plus people love it because it has all kinds of pretty analytics.

Sales tools

If you ever plan to sell something online you will need someone to handle either every part of the sales process or the most important part, moving the money.

To fully get the sales process we need to understand 3 things

1. The shop
2. The cart (optional)
3. The checkout

The shop is the software that shows people the products. This could be a full system or it could be just a picture on your page with some text under it.

Either way you need to show people what they're buying and how much it costs.

The cart is a collection of the things you want to buy at once. Many sales pages don't have a cart. They have a dedicated sales process and you can only buy that one product and its up sale products on that page. For now let's just assume we won't be using a cart.

The checkout is as you would imagine, where you pay and the money gets taken from your account and put into the sellers account.

The non techie options

One of the most popular and easy ways to get started selling anything online is through PayPal.

You've probably all used it before to buy things but did you can be on the shop side of things for free too? Well I say free they take 2.9% and 30c (USD) depending on your volume, it decreases as you process more sales.

They let you create a simple button that looks like this:

You set the price, you tell them if you want them to manage quantity, you set the page they will return to when they're done (your thank you page) and they give you the code to copy and paste.

It's pretty simple, no shop, no cart just checkout.

Ecwid is one of the coolest tools on the internet. They allow you to create a collection of products with them, set the price and off you go. They give you the code to embed the entire shop, cart and checkout into your site, it's pretty smooth!

What's more it's completely free for your first 10 products. It's only $15 (USD) a month if you want more and you can start to sell digital products too form just $15 a month.

That's pretty awesome if you ask me, the whole kit and kaboodal For nothing. If your just starting out and this is a great option.

For the techies

For those of you a little more comfortable with the code there's Stripe. The processing fees are the same as PayPal but it gives you a lot more control. If you're ok with getting your hands dirty in the code this is a very powerful platform.

They also have a shopping cart thing that you can put into your website like Ecwid, but to be honest I've never used it so I wouldn't know what to say about it.

For help automating your business talk to LandingPageGuys: https://landingpageguys.com/

They have a lot of experience working on automating people's sales funnels.

Summary

Automating your sales process is can be simple. If you've built your pales process the way I discussed in chapter 11 you've now doubt already figured out how to automate it.

The study of the journey from introduction to sale is the called Sales Funnels and working out what goes where to make the funnel more efficient is called funnel hacking.

There are some great tools to automate you sales process and you can use all in one solutions like Click Funnels or UnBounce or you can opt to build it yourself using webpages, email auto responders and sales tools.

Key Takeaways

- Work out the stages your customer takes
- Software tools can replace you in the sales process
- You can do it all for free and upgrade as you go

For more on Sales funnels check out https://foundr.com/automated-sales-funnel/

13 SHARPEN THE SWORD

When I was CTO of that tech company I mentioned earlier, I had convinced myself and others that I was the right man for the job. I had learned the 12 core competencies of my craft, I had built a compelling story based on my past experience and transferable skills. I even had a solution I could provide.

So why was I only there 6 months?

I made myself the person I needed to be to get that job. I branded myself as the expert in that field and I could do the job. So What was I missing?

For a start I was missing a rich business IT pedigree, I never went to some fancy business IT school. I hadn't spent years doing that job at other companies, but none of that mattered. The truth is I had become who I needed to be to do that job, but it doesn't end there.

The challenges of a company working on bleeding edge technology can't just be applied like a band aid and left to heal. This industry highlights the lifespan of a solution so well because the average lifespan of a solution in bleeding edge tech is about 3-6 months (if you're lucky).

In the 6 months I was working there, I saw a strong competitor come up in the first month, many more small players by the 3rd month and by month 6 everyone was racing to do what we hoped to achieve.

Turns out someone did succeed. About 4 months into my tenure, one of our competitors released a testing version of their platform. At the time, we were months away from even testing our software.

Moral was low at this point, not just with me but with the entire company. By this point the company had grown substantially, I had people under me looking for results, We had a fancy office in the heart of London's banking district and things were heating up.

Have you ever heard the expression "don't rest on your laurels"? It come from the Greek Olympian times. Winners of competitions would be given a sort of crown made of dark green leaves.

It's not known if this actually happened, but the idea is that these people would become complacent with their victory and they wouldn't train for the next race, as a result they became fatter and lazier and wouldn't win the race.

This is exactly what happened to me. I was living the dream life. A 6 figure salary (in pounds so it would be even more in USD), having custom made suits fitted for me, traveling to romantic European destinations every week with the then, love of my life.

As the months went on I grew complacent with my position, people looked up to me, but they also looked to me for newer and better solutions. I was so wrapped up in the joy of being where I wanted to be, that I didn't even notice everything else was falling apart.

My relationship at the time became neglected. I assumed everything was fine in my life and that extended to my personal life too. It all began to outgrow me.

I wasn't moving with the challenges, the problems were becoming harder and harder to solve, but I was just so happy that I'd solve the initial few problems.

By this point I knew that the reason the I wasn't keeping up with the challenges of the company was because I hadn't sharpened the sword. But I internalised it.

I made the problem about my self-worth. The worst thing you can do in times of trouble is adopt the fixed mindset.

I was reading about the fixed mindset in a book by Carol Dweck called mindset.

A fixed mindset believes that your DNA or your environment shapes who you are and you can never change, the growth mindset says that you have the ability to break the mould of your DNA and your upbringing and do what you want to do.

I like to think what Henry Ford said is true:

"Whether you believe you can or you can't, YOU'RE RIGHT!"

Being on the bleeding edge of something highlights just how quickly things change. Solutions can become obsolete in a heartbeat.

Fortunately if you're not working on bleeding edge technology, the average lifespan of a solution is a bit longer.

There are many factors that degrade and even destroy your solution, here are just a few examples:

- Time
- Leaks on sharing sites
- Competitors
- Changes to the tool
- Changes to the industry
- Changes to the economy

Time

No solution lasts forever, just as Robert Kiyosaki's 10 year old parables of wisdom are now common knowledge and my solutions to faster cryptocurrency transactions now practically industry standards. Any solution you create will eventually lose relevancy and or value. Something people are paying millions for today, will one day be given away free as someone's email gate, it's just the way it rolls.

Solution

There is no solution to time devalued content. You have to just create a new solution that continues to provide new value.

Leaks

This is just about the worst thing that can happen to content producer. This is the creative equivalent of theft. If you're content is duplicatable and distributable by people you haven't given permission to do so, then sooner or later they will devalue.

Everything on the internet is fair game. Sorry but it's true. There has never been a fool proof solution for serving content on the internet without someone very smart coming along and getting around it.

Wistia has gone to great lengths hide your original files from being downloaded. Their video player shows in the code the link to their website and their website knows where your file is. So the end user never sees the link to your original file on your page.

But follow those links long enough with a bit of technical knowledge and sure enough people will find them.

That's how the internet works. It was designed to be open. Unfortunately the is no way to make this open system 100% pay-per-view safe.

Solution

If this happens, you can still sell the content. Not everyone is tech savvy enough to steal your content and not everyone is tech savvy enough to go find it on sharing sites. But just know that it has devalued now, as a percentage of your audience can now get it for free.

Competitors

Ok so the reason why we become an expert in something isn't so we can know more than anyone else on the planet. It's so we can know enough to provide value. But there are people out there much farther along in providing solutions to your market than you are. So your top solution could be their introduction offer, or worse their email gate.

This isn't ideal and it's not what you signed up for. I promised you that you could start a business with at whatever level you're at and now I'm telling you that other people might be giving your solution away for free?

Ideally when you do your competitor analysis so you would be able to sniff out what they're providing for low value and you wouldn't be selling this as your solution.
But if you do end up in this position it can be hard to compete. Bigger more established experts just giving your solution away in exchange for someone's email or their introductory offer is not fun.

Solution

Fortunately you can prevent this by checking out the competition before you make your solution, but if you happened to miss this competitor or their offer then you can still charge people for it. Your personal twist on the solution could still add value.

Remember you bring your own personal flair to the solution, people are paying for your specific version of the solution. You might have more charisma than them, you might have better quality videos, you might have more of a hands on feel.

Many big competitors charge thousands of dollars to even take one of their online courses. If you're just starting out. You may be more available to your customers, you're not untouchable like them. Use that to your advantage.

Changes to the tool

I have taken courses on Social Media Marketing. I have produced courses on using Social Media for business. Just like Tia Lopez found out in his "new and improved Social Media" course, things change.

Those screenshots I took of my Facebook ads manager will likely be different if you're reading this 6 months from now. They may look completely different. Social Media sites are known for changing (a lot), some of them even go out of business.

When I was younger I knew HTML, JavaScript and CSS, the code you needed to make MySpace pages look good.

At the time it was huge a business selling themes for your MySpace profile. It never occurred to me to make the themes. That would have just seemed like too much work, but I did consider making courses on customizing your profile.

Turns out if I had done that, my solution would have been worthless just 3 months later. MySpace took a nose dive and the number of uses dropped drastically.

Many people made courses on how to advertise for SnapChat, how to make videos for Vine and so on. When the tool changes or disappears your solution will devalue.

Solution

Just like time there isn't really a solution to changes in the tools. I would avoid making content about specific tools because they change too much.

Changes to the industry

In 2017 it was all the rage to have your own Initial Coin Offering (ICO). These were made possible by a company called Ethereum. An ICO was a way for people to offer cryptocurrencies to people as a form of payment in advance on their new platform.

Kind of like Facebook tokens or in-game credits. You could buy them now, help fund the company and then you could pay-to-play with them when the product was ready.

This idea really appealed to me because I loved the idea of crow funding projects.

So I learned everything I could about ICOs and in a few months. I developed my 12 core competencies and I was ready to sell my services.

In the middle of 2018, just 6 months after the biggest cryptocurrency hype in history the financial authorities around the world declared that this was in breach of the laws made in the 1920s saying that only accredited investors (people with more than $1,000,000 USD net worth and $200,000+ annual income), were allowed to invest in these kinds of fund raising efforts. Your token also had to be registered as security too.

That meant you can't invest in this kind of thing unless it's registered and regulated by the financial authority of your country and you personally couldn't invest unless you were really rich.

This changed the industry what felt like overnight. Suddenly people were no longer looking to have these unregulated ICOs, but they wanted to stay compliant so something called a Security Token Offering (STO) was created.

An security token is cryptocurrency that has been registered with the local financial authorities and it has to represent some value like the shares in your company or a shared ownership in some real estate.

This meant that everything I had learned about ICOs was almost worthless. I had to learn this new method and how I could provide value as an expert here.

Solution

You could offer people historical education and advice about the industry, but that puts you in a different category. You're no longer an industry expert you're a historical expert. It has some value but not nearly as much and it's outside the scope of this book.

Changes to the economy

If you were trying to get hired in 2007-2009 you know just what effect changes in the economy can have on your business. Downturns, recessions, depressions and meltdowns highlight business models that are barely surviving.

"It's only when the tide goes out that you learn who has been swimming naked. "

Warren Buffet

This is a great quote which highlights the fact that anyone in business during the boom times who hasn't been paying attention to their clients, has been cutting costs or otherwise not providing the service they should have, stands out in the downturns.

If you are running a shoddy service, if your solution isn't what it's cracked up to be, yours will be the first people cut when times get tough.

Solution

If your solution has been devaluing for a while, it might be time to give it a revamp. Whether it's boomtimes or downturns, you need to make sure you're providing the best possible solution you can to your clients. If not when the downturn comes your service will be first on the chopping board.

Summery

I've spoken at industry leading events. I've held patents in my name and I've had large salaries. But I lost it all because I didn't sharpen the sword.

The value of your expertise is limited. Things will change, time will devalue your knowledge and skills, but that's ok. It just means it's time for you to step up and improve your game. Take the time improve the value of your solution and never rest on your laurels.

Key Takeaways

- Things change
- Your solution will devalue
- Review your solution at least every 6 months
- Improve your solution when you can

14 RINSE AND REPEAT

Well done, you made it all the way here. If you've followed all the advice and taken action on it you should have a fairly decent income stream now. All it needs now is for you to make it more efficient and scale up.

This book doesn't cover scaling, but if you're sharpening the sword often enough that's a good start. Learn more, become more valuable to your clients and get more clients.

An important thing to remember when scaling is your VRIN score. The VRIN score is the value of your solution.
It stand for:

1) Value
2) Rarity
3) Inimitable
4) Non-substitutional

Value

This one is pretty simple. How much value does your solution provide. Are you taking someone from 0-1? Have you got to the point now where your solution is multi-part and you can take someone from 0-1, then 2-20 and maybe even 6 figures to 7 figures.

How much is the most highly skilled appendix surgeon to you right now?

Unless you're currently in the peak of Appendicitis probably not much.

But how much is your morning coffee worth? To some people they can't function without it. So their productivity is thrown out and the day is lost. I'd say that was pretty valuable.

Your solution is as valuable as opportunity loss and the opportunity gain it shields your from or provides.

If you can't recognise the value you bring to your clients then you're losing money.

Rarity

This is exactly what it says on the tin. How many other people are capable of providing this solution. Not just exactly like yours but anyone who can achieve the same results.

Remember our surgeon friend from before?

If you ever find yourself on a desert island with an appendix on the verge of explosion that doctors resident assistant will become infinitely more valuable than his mentor is to you right now.

If you're the only person in your village, town or city who can provide people with that solution your business will scale quicker than you'll likely know what to do with.

That's a good problem to have. Because you can pay other people to figure that out for you at this point (Oh by the way, if that is you, we should to talk).

Inimitable

This one sounds kinda hard but it's really not. This just means how possible is it for others to copy you?

If you're don't have some form of protection against copying both technical and legal, someone will copy you. Someone could download your content and give it away for free, someone could go through your content and decide they want to start teaching exactly that in the same way.

Licensing is a great way to make sure unauthorised people don't copy you. It also allows you to create a way in which to certify people in your training methods. You can charge people to train in your method and you can also charge people a percentage of their earning to practice or promote themselves on your website.

This is sometimes called franchising.

Immutability can work against you or with you if done well.

Non-substitutional

You know how you really love the soft smooth feeling of the luxury brand of toilet paper? It sucks when you have to use that rough store brand version huh?

But you can still use it though, because you need to. That makes it substitutional.

Velcro! A company in America owns the exclusive rights to sell all Velcro in the world! It's true. If you want to make a coat with Velcro on it, you have to go through them, or at least the manufacturers of your coat do.

If you need to have Velcro on your product, there is literally no one else in the world who is allowed to manufacture and sell you that Velcro.

Does this mean it doesn't happen? Hell now, there are thousands of copies of it here in Asia but that's beside the point.
Anyone wishing to make a coat that uses Velcro and wants to sell in the 5 major English speaking countries of the world legally has to go through them.

Officially, there is no substitutional brand.

A good start at scaling your business is to improve your VRIN score. Add value to your solution. Add parts that no one else can copy. Franchise the solution out and make it vital that your customers come to you over someone else and your business will surely scale.

Repeat

You can choose to scale this business up and focus only on this business, but why? There is so much more possibilities and so many more businesses you can make if you learn to create new solutions.

Why stop with just one solution, you are infinitely creative and now have the tools to learn a new industry, create a solution to its problems and sell them on autopilot. You can have an army of solutions working for you, providing value to your customers and adding a new income stream to your bank account.

A word on setbacks

There will be times where you learn all the 12 core competencies, brand a perfect solution, find people who will want it, automate and even improve then you might not get the results that you want.

Remember, there is no such thing as failure, only results. Sometimes you might not like those results, sometimes you will lose money on those results and even fold businesses based on those results, but it's not the end of the world.

That's why we build multiple streams of income.

Your income stream may not last forever. It may not even get off the ground. You may have to give refunds and that sucks because it means you sold someone a solution that wasn't right for them.

There will always be a percentage of people who don't bother to go through your products at all. A percentage of people who are indifferent to your solution and a percentage of people who will excel using it.

That's just how it works. Not everyone who buys your solution will use it, not everyone who uses your solution will understand it and not everyone who understands it will love it.

That's just part of the expert business.

So don't quite your job until you're 100% sure your business is ready to scale. Don't move on, to a new income stream until the last one is on autopilot and never, ever give up on your dreams.

This is what freedom feels like

Congratulations, you now have all the tools you need to create the life of your dreams, you now hold the knowledge and skills to create financial freedom for yourself and your family.

From this moment on your life can be as awesome as you want it to be. Remember the reason we do this is to spend time with our loved ones and living our lives. So go out there and start your story.

Travel the world, meet new people, write a book, leave a legacy. Never be controlled by money ever again because you now have the power to make money your subordinate and that is true freedom.

Thank you for taking the time to read my book and I hope it brings you the success and happiness it has me.

DISCLAIMER

The author of this book makes no claims on earnings, the results of the author has seen are not typical and depend on the input of the reader.

The author takes no responsibility for risk or loss of money, time or any other resource cause by the actions of the reader as a result of reading this book.

This information is provided for educational and informational purposes.

The author is not a registered financial or legal advisor and offers no advice on either.

The income experienced by the author and his clients are not typical. The author and the publisher take no responsibility for the reader not achieving their goals.

By reading this book the reader accepts responsibility for his or her own actions and results.

Bibliography

List of industries
https://www.bls.gov/iag/tgs/iag_index_alpha.htm

Robert Kiyosaki your house is not an asset.
https://www.amazon.co.uk/Rich-Dad-Poor-Teach-Middle/dp/1612680011

VRIN score by Tai Lopez
https://www.tailopezsmma.com/11-secrets-to-making-money-with-internet-marketing/

Seth Godin people like us do things like this
https://www.youtube.com/watch?v=rdUeq09cGJ0

Color psychology
https://en.wikipedia.org/wiki/Color_psychology